THE
SUBSTANCE
OF FIRE

THE SUBSTANCE OF FIRE

A Screenplay by
Jon Robin Baitz

based on his play

New York

ISBN 0-7868-8256-5

Designed by Nancy Singer

For Ron & Iva, with love
(All writers should have such friends to ply them with wine
at lunch, and make them laugh at dinner.)

ACKNOWLEDGMENTS

From the first reading of the play to the final day of shooting the movie, I was blessed with the good fortune of working with true friends, from the awe-inspiring Dan Sullivan, to a group of extraordinary actors, and I would be remiss were I not to take this space to thank at least *some* of them. They include: Rob Morrow, Gina Gershon, Bradley White, Rose Gregorio, and Merrill Holtzman, who helped coax a play out of some slim scraps of writing. Patrick Breen, John Tenney, John Hickey, Cordelia Richards, and Maria Tucci will always have my gratitude for their extraordinary work at Playwrights Horizons and Lincoln Center, which brings me to Andre Bishop and Bernard Gersten, two Medicis of Manhattan. Finally, George Lane, Michael Peretzian, Arnold Rifkin, and Ron Kastner, producers in name *or* spirit: Without them, there would have been no picture.

INTRODUCTION

Like many playwrights, I find the film world both starkly inhospitable, and glitteringly alluring all at once. For me, the trick to screenwriting is to balance the two avocations and step back and forth between them; dual citizenship intact. In this role I find myself doing an almost an impossible dance—like a Hassid doing Bunraku; culturally and emotionally I have the temperature of a playwright. The problems of adjusting to a language of images over sentences goes counter to all that I have absorbed and instinctualized in the theatre.

To write a screenplay is to come face-to-face with a conundrum: An ironclad (but as yet, mercifully *unwritten*) set of secret edicts appears to dominate what is thought of as "good" American script writing; brittle, tightly observed rules, all having to do with forward motion, short, taciturn bursts of dialogue; very little silence, (broken mostly by gunfire); and the occasional sly slipping in of a cinder block of words—an island of language—to counter the unstoppable flow of pictures on the screen. To make it worse, there are these conventions regarding something called the three-act structure even though real stories consist of act after act, tumbling and falling and crossing one another like music, and then dying down. (Think of Mahler or Stravinsky). Traditional notions of what constitutes a solid screenplay involve setting up events, making them pay off later; measuring when to resolve what story line; in other words, a large part of it is mathematics. Playwriting seems to me the very opposite of screenwriting: One keeps going *at* an idea, chipping away at its surface, not much concerned with how claustrophobic or "confined" something might be. One keeps looking for new approaches to the thing.

So these two modes of writing are basically at war with one another. When the playwright in me sat down to adapt *Substance*, he did real battle with the screenwriter. There were extended periods of exhausted paralysis, baffled scribbling, and slack-jawed peering at blank pages. If I was able to bring those two worlds to a truce, it's only because Dan Sullivan was there as a peacekeeping force: We sat across from each other and he wrote as much as I did and like the gentleman he is, refused to take credit for it.

I spent most of 1989–1990 writing the play, but the actual physical work of getting pen to paper occurred over two nights some six months apart; both acts written in a lovely borrowed house (Ron Rifkin and his wife, Iva's), in the Hollywood hills, where I was in exile from Manhattan, trying to knock out a screenplay about a volatile theater couple's final battle royale, ending in double murder. (For *Disney!* Unproducable, needless to say. I still sigh at the thought of those meetings with the helpful, increasingly less hopeful, openhearted executives trying to assist a lost cause, like ER medics working on a fading octogenarian smoker.)

The play came straight out of an attempt to write myself out of the blues: The Isaac Geldhart of the second act pretty much reflected the dislocation, the scarring depression I felt myself to be laboring under. I was trying to capture the dangerously inevitable downward spiral that at the time I felt lay at the heart of all human business. And in retrospect, I was praying for some leavening of that despair: *The Substance of Fire* was secretly about a quest for passion and belief.

Sometimes writing can make things slightly better: You get to put form to the shape in the darkness, to give it a name. That helps. And being a playwright, if you're lucky, you eventually get to be surrounded by actors and directors and stuff. Lighting people, cigarette breaks. It's all very low-tech and comforting. You don't have to go it *alone*. So starving for contact with others, I finally finished the play. Nervously, I sent it to New York ahead of me, to my friends at Naked Angels, the theater company I was part of, and after some enthusiastic beckoning gestures from Back East (the kind you use to lure a dog into a lake), I followed home, to a little emotional rescue party, as it were. And so began the long haul that eventually ended with the film version, which is quite different from the play; cleaner, more direct; a movie. The screenplay looks for narrative where there was only inference and mood in the stage version. This is an adjustment, and one I was happy to make. I am working still to make my peace with the screenwriter's secret rulebook, (or rebel against it where I can), and have started to even appreciate the formal rigors of the craft. (An appreciation of twentieth-century German architecture helps. Perhaps that of Albert Speer.)

I think, though, working with friends and loved ones on a small scale, as we did on this picture, is the easiest way to learn: If we failed at "professional" (by which I mean Hollywood) filmmaking, we still want to all work together again, and fail even better. From sitting in a hotel room in Seattle, improvising lines with Dan Sullivan, to watching Sarah Jessica Parker and Ron Rifkin reinvent parts they had helped to create, it was good to work outside the studio system and not have experts on hand to remind us of the rules of the game. It felt like the two worlds of theater and film sort of came together for a bit. A happy marriage.

I should note my spotty history as a screenwriter. Prior to adapting *Substance of Fire*, and after the Disney episode, I had done a few drafts of a remake of Sinclair Lewis's *Dodsworth*, but childishly chaffed at getting notes from studio executives who instead of putting their names to them, hid behind "We," as in "We feel it's too much of a *downer*." I should have been grown-up enough to take their money *and* their manners in stride, but was spoilt by the autonomy of being a playwright. I was younger. After *Dodsworth*, I tried an adaptation of a Somerset Maugham novella, which I couldn't crack, but then again, neither could the writer who preceeded me, one Christopher Isherwood. (Maugham apparently wrote *Up at the Villa* in less than a week, to fulfill a contractional obligation to what was then called, in 1941, a woman's magazine.) The producers were philosophical about it. ("After all, if Maugham had only taken a week to write it, how good could it *be*?") We're still friends. That was followed by an adaptation of a slim Jim Thompson story that Tom Cruise directed for Showtime's *Fallen Angels* noir anthology series. I am currently adapting a Robert Penn Warren novel, *Meet Me in the Green Glen*. I rather like this work. It is merely a profession, whereas playwriting is an addiction. I hope I've learned some of the tricks along the way. To quote from Robert

Stone's wonderful Hollywood novel, *Children of Light*, in which an on-the-ropes screenwriter defends his profession to a jealous journalist: "You have to believe it's worthwhile, and you have to accept the rules. You can't be a solitary or an obsessive. You can't despise your audience. It requires humility and it requires strength of character." Wise words.

Jon Robin Baitz
Sag Harbor, New York

THE
SUBSTANCE
OF FIRE

INT. AN ATTIC, MIDDLE EUROPE, 1939

ANGLE FROM BEHIND ON A SIX-YEAR-OLD BOY sitting on a cot, reading a book. The only light in the room emanates from a tiny lamp. A board-covered window beyond. A neat attic. Neat piles of books surround the boy in this boy's home. The sound of an EXCITED CROWD from the street below.

ANGLE ON THE BOY going to the window, his face always hidden from us. We hear splintering wood, breaking glass, yelling, etc. The boy cautiously pulls back the boards.

EXT. EUROPEAN STREET. TWILIGHT/DAY:

BOY'S POV: A bonfire in the middle of a cobblestone street. Ashes and embers and flames fly up into the dusk. The bonfire is of household furniture, books are being tossed into the flames. Ashes blown by the wind up toward him. Only the tops of heads, from above. A FAMILY—PARENTS, TWO BOYS, AND A LITTLE GIRL are being led away by GERMAN SOLDIERS. More books are thrown on the fire.

EXT. EUROPEAN STREET. TWILIGHT/DAY:

ANGLE FROM BEHIND A WOMAN tossing books into the bonfire.

ANGLE ON the smoke and bits of paper as they fly up into the sky. The CAMERA MOVES UP with the debris and finds the BOY at the attic window and dimly discerns his eyes peering through a gap in the boards. He holds his hand out and into the column of smoke carefully, the way one tests water temperature.

ANGLE ON BOY FROM STREET *with his hand reaching out, silhouetted against the sky.*

ANGLE ON BOY FROM OUTSIDE WINDOW LOOKING IN. *He catches a charred bit of a burnt book, and quickly withdraws his hand.*

EXT. ATTIC WINDOW. TWILIGHT/DAY.

The boy's eyes peering out, as smoke, rising up, fills the frame.

INT. PRINTER'S SHOP. NEW YORK CITY. DAY. PRESENT.

The SOUND of a printing press. THE CAMERA pans very tightly around a working press, and stops at the face of ISAAC GELDHART as he stares down in deep concentration. Isaac, a man in his early sixties in suit and tie, is examining different printings on various papers. He considers thickness, width, texture. OTTO, his production manager, and an ANCIENT PRINTER in a blue ink-covered smock, watch him. In the background is a large press. The ancient printer holds the paper up to the window; sunlight filters through.

> ISAAC
> Not quite right, is it? Well, sort of . . .

He looks at them, a not unsympathetic expression of distaste on his face. They nod and sigh: This is not the unexpected response. He reaches for a similar, stained, printer's smock and slips it over his suit.

> ISAAC
> Like a book for rich men who hate books. It's not heavy
> enough for the trim size of the page.

He puts down the paper and spreads it open before them. He rubs his hand along the printed type on the page.

> ISAAC
>
> It should be rougher.

> PRINTER
>
> Rougher? Rougher than this?

> ISAAC
>
> You want to feel the type pushing in.

> PRINTER
>
> We don't have the machines for that.

> ISAAC
>
> You don't need it.

What follows are a series of intricate shots of the printing process. Over the TITLE CREDITS, we see a page of a book being made.

BEGIN OPENING TITLE SEQUENCE

VARIOUS SHOTS OF ISAAC

Masterfully working with the equipment. The title page being printed is The Architecture of the Holocaust. *Isaac examines it and closely holds it up to the light. Isaac goes to the press, upon which sits a sheet of blank paper. It is smaller than the first piece. He dabs water onto it. Isaac turns to the printer and motions for him to activate the press, which he does.*

ANGLE ON A PAGE BEING PRINTED: The men stare down at the wet, glistening letters, the words, the layout.

END OPENING TITLE SEQUENCE

> ISAAC

Closer.

> OTTO

Gonna get expensive.

> ISAAC

Perfecto.

EXT. PARK AVENUE. DAY.

ANGLE ON ISAAC walking downtown on Park Avenue. He holds the book-box, hurrying.

ANGLE ON ISAAC as he arrives at the Kreeger/Geldhart building. He opens the glass door to the building as CORA CAHN, a woman in her fifties, simultaneously exits the building. She looks at him in recognition.

> CORA

Isaac . . .

He looks at her with a slightly alarmed, mostly neutral expression.

> CORA
> *(nervous)*

It's Cora Cahn. It's so good to see you again. I was on the

library committee with your wife. I was so sorry to hear about her—she was a wonderful, wonderful—I've been through it too, you know, ah, the loneliness—

ISAAC
(rhythmically nodding and smiling, trapped now)
Yes, well, thank you very much. Now if you'll excuse . . .

He tries to walk past her.

CORA
We wrote you a note—the library committee—Wouldn't you like to take Rena's place on the preservation committee in her memory? It would mean so much. It would mean so much to us, you know, to keep the Geldhart name.

At some point during the above speech, Isaac has leaned against the wall, holding the book-box to his chest as though for protection. He looks longingly at the elevator bank.

INT. KREEGER/GELDHART PUBLISHERS. MANHATTAN. DAY.

A building in the Flatiron district. AARON GELDHART in the board-room/library with two JAPANESE FINANCIERS, The OTANI family—a father in his sixties and his son. Aaron is the sort of young man who favors discreet, though flagrantly expensive, suits; behind him are bookcases; locked behind glass are first editions of K/G books going back to the early twenties.

On the table between Aaron and the Otanis is a pile of books representing the publishing house's output the previous season. In front of the Otanis are financial printouts: The Otanis don't look impressed. They shouldn't.

AARON

My father is still the single most important publisher of serious
work in this country. In my opinion.

He indicates the volumes on the table between them.

AARON

The Burning Sky—Art from the Spanish Civil war. That's a . . .
big . . .

*He opens a page. A horrific black and white of a burnt woman circa 1936
Madrid. The Japanese look squeamish. He quickly closes the book, picks
up another.*

AARON

Craters and Mounds. An anthology of poetry by political pris-
oners in the Third World. We won an Amnesty Award for . . .
or Unesco . . .

*The Japanese are silent. Mr. Otani looks down at the ledger. The son ex-
amines the eraser on his lacquered pencil.*

AARON
(bucking up)
Water on Fire: An Oral History of the Children of Hiroshima
. . . That—would you like a copy of that?

*He slides an impressive book across the table toward the Otanis, who have
a sort of collective poker face.*

OTANI JUNIOR
Mr. Geldhart. The list of books, are, truly somewhat . . .

AARON

Yes, I know, I know, you'd have to call them serious.

OTANI SENIOR

"Morbid" is the word, actually.

AARON
(stiff)

Look, we are well aware of the financial burden on subject matters which are . . . err—

OTANI JNR.

The numbers are not terribly encouraging. Kreeger/Geldhart Publishing desperately needs to diversify its list, Mr. Geldhart.

Aaron swallows back his acrid embarrassment and puts his best foot forward.

AARON

I couldn't agree with you more, that's why we're planning to move into a new phase. New ideas, new subjects. Life now. Today's complexities.
(beat)
You're turning down our loan.
(beat)
We are prepared to offer you exclusive worldwide rights to our entire backlist in exchange for the loan. I mean, when you think about the whole world, surely there's someone out there who gets this.

Aaron indicates Water On Fire. *The Japanese look at the cover, impassive, not biting.*

INT. ELEVATOR. KREEGER/GELDHART. DAY.

The doors open on the Kreeger/Geldhart floor. ANGLE ON ISAAC getting off. A WPA craftsman-style mural covers the walls of the entrance to Kreeger/Geldhart.

INT. K/G PUBLISHERS. HALLWAY/FOYER. DAY.

ANGLE ON MISS BARZAKIAN, a "handsome" woman. As reception-ist–majordomo, she keeps traffic flowing at Kreeger/Geldhart. She works from behind a small desk in the foyer. A MAN sits, waiting for Isaac.

> BARZAKIAN
> *(rises to greet Isaac with his messages)*
> Louis is in your office.

> ISAAC
> *(panic, moans)*
> You didn't give him my edits did you?

> BARZAKIAN
> *(rolls her eyes)*
> I heard him yelling, so watch out.

> ISAAC
> My God, couldn't you at least stall him? How long's he been
> in there?

> BARZAKIAN
> You're only two hours late.

ANGLE ON AARON leading the Japanese out of the boardroom, and ushering them past Isaac, who raises his eyebrows at Aaron, who shakes his head "not now" as they make their way out to the elevator. Isaac watches.

INT. KREEGER/GELDHART PUBLISHERS. HALLWAY/FOYER. DAY.

ANGLE ON and POV ISAAC watching Aaron at the elevator door with the Otanis.

> AARON
>
> I think this was a good first meeting, gentlemen. An open dis-
> cussion, right? Mr. Otani, I want to thank you.

> ISAAC
>
> Aaron—when you have a moment—please—

> AARON
>
> Mr. Otani, I really want to thank you. Your advice was sage,
> and anyone would do well to follow it.

INT. KREEGER/GELDHART. ELEVATOR BANK. DAY.

The Otanis and Aaron wait for the elevator. It opens, discharging VAL CHENARD and his agent, GENE BYCK. The Otanis get in.

> AARON
> *(to the Otanis, eager to see them go)*
> Good-bye. Thanks! Boy. Really. You were just—
> *(turns to Chenard)*
> Hey, I'll be right with you.
> *(to Otanis)*

Thank you so much again. I hope you—yeah—
                    (to Chenard)
Hi.

Val Chenard is handsome; a scruffed-up downtown guy in Doc Martin boots and old black torn jeans and all that. BYCK tends toward pinstripes and glasses.

CHENARD
                    (laughing nervously, points to Byck)
Hi. This is-this-this is—

BYCK

Gene Byck.

Aaron laughs in recognition.

AARON

Sure, I know Gene.

BYCK

What's the skinny?

CHENARD

He thought he should come along.

AARON
                    (ushering in, a little worn)
So. You got an agent.

CHENARD

Well, this morning—

BYCK

I'm over the moon about this book.

AARON

Yeah, so am I.

INT. BOARDROOM. DAY.

Isaac is escorting LOUIS FOUKOLD, an ancient scholar, down the stairs from his office. Louis holds a massive manuscript. Isaac is piling loose pieces of it onto Louis's pile.

ISAAC

Louis, please. This is not your clubhouse. It's my office. Come right over here and sit down.

LOUIS

Who gave you permission to edit this material? All I can see is red.

ISAAC

Louis, I'm trying to do you a favor. You bring me five thousand pages. Now you tell me, who would publish such a thing?

INT. K/G PUBLISHERS. AARON'S OFFICE. DAY.

Aaron is looking at Val. Byck is being an agent. Aaron is straight-faced.

BYCK

(holding up a manuscript entitled Rising Tide— *by Val Chenard)*
(he laughs)
You have no idea. It's lunatic. My phone is ringing off the—

Harry Fitzhugh from Knopf is screaming into my voice mail.
We're talking Anne Rice numbers, Aaron. Now come on.
Humor me.

> *(beat)*

I mean. This is not what you guys do well.

AARON

So, what do we guys do well, Gene?

BYCK

> *(unblinking)*

If I had a book that was really, really depressing . . . like a novel
set in a kibbutz or a mangrove swamp or an oral history of the
wives of Mexican muralists. Val's book is a funny, smart, so-
phisticated, contemporary take on the zeitgeist.

AARON

> *(shakes his head at Gene)*

I'm not doing this with you.

He turns to Val.

BYCK

Everyone in this town knows your company's on the ropes,
Aaron. I mean, those guys in the elevator are not here for a
Ping-Pong championship. Can you play in this game?

AARON

Val, could I talk to you alone for a minute? Please? Phoebe,
would you fix Byck something to drink?

Val looks at Byck and smiles. Byck shrugs, a "what's the harm" gesture.

Byck rises and walks out of the office into the hallway. Gene Byck is sil-houetted in the glass panes behind Val and Aaron.

AARON

I mean why would you bring your agent?

VAL

He's an agent, he's not literally my agent, he's an agent at an agency.

AARON

That man is the angel of death.

VAL

He said I had a voice.

AARON

You do have a voice, Val. It happens to be annoying me right now, but you do have a voice.

VAL

He loved the book—he just wanted to be around it.

AARON

He just wanted to be around it? He actually said that?

VAL

I didn't know this guy was going to turn into Meyer Lansky. Look, if I did anything offensive—it's that—I don't know. I don't know what I'm doing.

AARON

I didn't need to—to get involved. Jesus.

Val reaches over and strokes Aaron's hand. The hair on his wrist. Aaron looks down, then looks over at Byck: Byck has caught this. He shakes his head.

AARON

Oh, great.

INT. K/G PUBLISHERS. ISAAC'S OFFICE. DAY.

Aaron enters with the Chenard manuscript under his arm. Isaac is at his work table with the proofs he's brought back from the printer's.

AARON
(hands him the Chenard)
Read it tonight. Everybody's after this. He's off to Knopf if we say no.

ISAAC
So that's the kid with the big black Frankenstein shoes? Tell me what happened, you meet him at the disco?

AARON
(sort of smiling, an old routine)
What does that mean?

ISAAC
You gotta be a particular kind of guy to wear rivets on your shoes.

AARON
(used to this)
Yeah, yeah. You have a true sociopath's eye for footwear, Pop.

ISAAC

The bigger the shoe, the smaller the book.
(Aaron looks at him)

Aaron starts out, passes the proofs on the table of The Architecture of the Holocaust.

AARON

What's this?

ISAAC

That's the I.G. Farben book. Just a first go at it.

Aaron looks down at the thing, and back up at Isaac. A gesture of, "Are you kidding me?"

ISAAC

It's a limited edition.

AARON

A limited edition of the Farben?

He fingers the paper, knowing its cost, moaning, and looks at Isaac.

ISAAC

A commemorative edition.

AARON

Commemorative? Of what? Of having sold seventeen copies?

LOUIS

(enters and interrupts. He holds up the edits he's examining. Shock.)
What is this? How dare you cut one scintilla of my book?

AARON

Louis, we're in the middle of a discussion—

ISAAC

(going over to Louis)

Scintilla? Louis, did you use the word "scintilla" with me?

AARON

Dad—

LOUIS

There's nothing left of the experiments by Mengele on twins!

AARON

(losing Isaac)

Please. Please . . . Can we . . . ?

ISAAC

(ignoring Aaron, crosses to Louis)

I'm trying to help you, Louis, okay?

Isaac follows Louis out of the office. Aaron looks after them in dismay.

AARON

Can't we ever finish a conversation in this office?

EXT. STREET. GRAMERCY PARK. AFTERNOON.

Isaac walks along Gramercy Park North, turns along the side of the park, to Gramercy Park South. He has an umbrella in his hand. He stands for a moment, watching the empty park. He imperiously steps out into the street, indifferent to whatever vehicular traffic is in his way (in this case, a

*taxi). He places his umbrella against the front bumper of the taxi, as it
SCREECHES to a halt.*

*ANGLE ON ISAAC entering his brownstone apartment, which overlooks
the park.*

INT. ISAAC'S APARTMENT. GRAMERCY PARK. AFTERNOON.

*A vast, high-ceilinged brownstone living room overlooking the park. The
walls are dominated by floor-to-ceiling bookshelves. Isaac sits at his desk.
The television is on. A YOUNG WOMAN is singing on a children's pro-
gram. She dances with someone in a big chicken suit, who squawks and
clucks. Isaac picks up the phone, dials. It rings. He puts on the speaker-
phone as phone continues to RING.*

INT. MARTIN'S HOUSE. LIVING ROOM. AFTERNOON.

*ANGLE ON MARTIN'S DESK. The phone is ringing. The CAMERA
moves past his desk to the window beyond, toward trees outside.*

CUT TO:

EXT. VASSAR COLLEGE. AFTERNOON.

*A MOVING SHOT. The CAMERA moves toward trees with landscape
beyond.*

*MARTIN GELDHART and a small group of students sit under a tree.
They are STEWART, RACHEL, and KEVIN. An idyllic setting. Back-*

17

packs and silence, just the chirping of birds. They all look around. Kevin is drawing what they see: this pastoral place.

MARTIN

Time's up. So. What's missing?

STEWART

(knows he's wrong)

You need a foreground?

MARTIN

No, Stewart, that's art class. Think Olmstead, think how he transformed nature. So. What's missing?

What is the one thing that all landscape architecture requires?

There is a silence. Martin gets up and walks toward the trees, smiling.

RACHEL

There has to be a social motive?

MARTIN

(encouragingly)

Yes, yes . . . so . . . it needs . . . us!

He begins running toward the meadow, turns back to look at the kids. They start laughing.

MARTIN

It doesn't work without us! It needs us!

Stewart, Rachel, and Kevin laugh. Kevin starts to add a figure to his landscape drawing. Martin strikes a heroic pose. The students smile affectionately.

INT. MARTIN'S HOUSE. POUGHKEEPSIE. EVENING.

Martin sits at a drawing table. Three or four students in the background. Some working at projects, others talking and laughing. DR. JOHN rolls out of the speakers, booming and warm and funky, like the house itself. A rare white orchid sits on the windowsill in front of Martin. He is completing a beautiful botanical rendering of it. The phone by Martin's drawing table is RINGING. The ringing phone is finally picked up by Stewart. He comes to Martin.

                    STEWART

    It's your dad.

Martin shakes his head, no.

INT. ISAAC'S HOUSE. LIVING ROOM. EVENING.

A wide shot. The television is now off. Isaac is holding the phone.

                    ISAAC
                (into the phone)
    Uh-huh. Uh-huh.

From the other end of the phone, Dr. John can be heard, playing faintly. Isaac hangs up, clearly a little hurt. He glances down at an illustrated letter lying on his desk.

INT. KREEGER/GELDHART PUBLISHERS. AARON'S OFFICE. DAY.

Isaac smiles and goes into Aaron's office. He drops the Chenard on the desk in front of him.

19

ISAAC

Well, lucky us. Another book we don't have to publish. Boy,
am I telling you, this thing—

Isaac laughs.

AARON
(surprised)

What?

ISAAC

The book is crapola, we'll have the last laugh.

AARON

Wait a minute.

ISAAC

So, next.

Isaac smiles and swiftly walks out.

AARON

Dad! Dad!

INT. KREEGER/GELDHART PUBLISHERS. HALLWAY OUTSIDE
AARON'S OFFICE. DAY.

*Isaac walks quickly, carrying a letter in his hand. Aaron follows him into
the hallway.*

AARON

Dad, look, we can't pass on this, we have to publish it. It's going to be a big book, it's going to do big numbers, it's good, we have to.

Isaac is at the copy machine and copies the letter.

> ISAAC
> We *have* to? Tell me, Aaron, tell me why, exactly why do *we* have to.

INT. COPY ROOM. DAY.

Aaron follows Isaac to the copy machine. Aaron looks at Isaac for a moment, and shakes his head, smiling.

> AARON
> Because we do.

> ISAAC
> Because it's filled with poetry? Because it's deeply ironic?

Isaac copies the letter.

> What did you think?

> AARON
> Oh, boy.

> ISAAC
> Aaron, what's the big deal? It's a lousy book.

> AARON
> It's not lousy.

ISAAC

Please, forget about the manuscript, will you? Just . . . stick to
the money problems.

ANGLE ON ISAAC *starting back down the hall, followed by Aaron.*
IN THE HALLWAY: Isaac and Aaron arrive at Miss Barzakian's desk.
Isaac summarily exits into the boardroom, Aaron following.
IN THE BOARDROOM: Isaac and Aaron enter the boardroom. Louis is
at the table.

AARON

You asked me to come on here, Dad.
(beat)
We are hemorrhaging money. What are we going to do? Please,
tell me. Do you have an idea?

There is a moment. Isaac sighs and shrugs. Hesitates.

ISAAC

Yes, I'm going to publish this.

He indicates Louis's work.

AARON

This?

ISAAC

Yes, four volumes on the Nazi medical experiments. That's it.
We're going to put everything behind it.

AARON

Are you seriously proposing this to me?

ISAAC

I'm not proposing anything, Aaron, I've decided.

AARON

You've decided? This will sink us.
    (softly)
Are you sure you don't want to discuss this with me? Find a
way to do both . . . ?

ISAAC

I am quite sure, thank you, Aaron.
    (beat. Aaron is about to speak. Isaac has had enough)
Thank you, Aaron.

*Aaron exits the boardroom. He stands, looking at Miss Barzakian. Aaron
stands in the hall, thinking. Miss Barzakian looks at him.*

BARZAKIAN

    (over Isaac and Louis; helpful but knows it's not)
Aaron, this too shall pass.

INT. TV STUDIO. DAY.

*Aaron enters with manuscript. He watches SARAH GELDHART and a
young man in a cow suit, PETER, rehearse a teaching song about the letter
"c". MAX, the director, is above in his booth.*

SARAH

    (singing)
If your "c" is not quite correct, if you try but you can't quite
connect . . .
    (continuing)

Don't cry if you don't know how to make a "c" . . . If you wanna know how, call the cow. Call the cow, call the cow, call the cow.

MAX
Thank you, perfect, but Sarah, Sarah—

SARAH
Call the cow . . . Moo!

MAX
(over Sarah, interrupting)
Sarah . . . Sarah . . . I'm sorry to interrupt you again—

SARAH
Can I just get through it once, Max? I'll never get it.

MAX
There's a little filigree in there on—
(singing)
Cor-rect!
(speaking)
You hear it.
Con-nect.

SARAH
Okay.

MAX
And you don't need to tart it up with a lot of head wagging.

SARAH
I didn't know I . . . I mean.

MAX
Relax. Let the words do the work.

Sarah does neck exercises.

PETER

Max, do I have to wear the nose?

MAX

(to Peter)

Actually, yes. Peter dear, your moo's sounding a bit consumptive. She's a healthy, happy cow.

Max notices Aaron.

MAX

(to Aaron; through mike)

Excuse me, sir, would you mind just stepping out for a bit? No visitors. It's hard with visitors.

Sarah looks up at the booth.

SARAH

(to Max)

Max, he's my brother.

She turns to Peter.

SARAH

(to Peter)

That's my brother.

PETER

(to Aaron; as though saying "hi")

Moo.

EXT. STREET. OUTSIDE STUDIO. DAY.

The doors fling open and a young dog, EMILY, a golden retriever on a leash, followed by Sarah, and the show's director, MAX. Aaron struggles to keep up.

SARAH

I'm not rushing, the dog is pulling. Come on. Emily. Emily. Stay! . . . is there a command for slow?

MAX

Have you tried arsenic, dear?

SARAH

Sweetie. Emily loves you!
        (to the dog)
Hey! Slower! Emily! Can we . . . slow down!

AARON
       (handing her the manuscript)
I'm just asking you to read it, Sarah.

SARAH
       (over the barking dog)
Aaron, please. Why do I always have to be the tiebreaker? Look, I have to get Emily home and we're going to . . .

She looks at Max.

SARAH

What are we going to?

MAX

Tristan and Isolde, love.

SARAH
(*"can you believe it?"*)

I thought I hated opera.

AARON

Yeah, but we've got to do something. Mom left us her shares of this company, and we have a responsibility. Really, it's your company, Sarah.

Sarah, exasperated, takes the manuscript. Max has hailed a cab and is holding the door. Emily jumps in.

AARON

Thank you.

SARAH

I told you. We warned you. Martin and I warned you not to go work there. Remember?

AARON

Please don't do "I told you so."

Sarah smiles, kisses Aaron.

SARAH

I told you so.

Aaron laughs, ruefully.

MAX

We're late.

Sarah gets in the cab and leans out the window, looks at Aaron.

SARAH

I'll read it. Get a life.

INT. METRO NORTH TRAIN APPROACHING MANHATTAN. DAY.

Martin sits staring at the approaching urban scene. Beside him sits the Chenard manuscript. He is deep in thought.

INT. DOCTOR KRAMER'S OFFICE. MANHATTAN. DAY.

Martin sits reading the Chenard manuscript. A YOUNG NURSE takes blood.

NURSE
(preparing to draw blood)
You had Hotchkins, huh?

MARTIN

Uh-huh.

NURSE

Full remission, that's lucky.
(She sticks the needle in his arm. Martin turns a page of the manuscript, laughing at what he's reading. Beat.)

MARTIN

Yeah, I guess.

NURSE

Trust me, that's lucky.

DOCTOR BART KRAMER, sixty-six, friendly, enters.

NURSE

You still get tired?

DR. KRAMER

Of course he's tired. He's the son of Isaac Geldhart.

He leans against the counter observing Martin.

MARTIN

Look doc, no bruises.

DR. KRAMER

I'm not kidding about this . . .

The nurse has drawn one tube of blood. With the needle still intact in Martin's arm, she begins to draw a second tube.

MARTIN

I check my little body every day.

DR. KRAMER

Nursie tells me you've lost a little weight, that's a no-no, Martin.

MARTIN
(to nurse)

Could you maybe leave me enough blood to get home or something?

DR. KRAMER

You do look a little run-down.

MARTIN

Who'd have thought remission was as big a pain in the ass as the disease itself?

The second tube is now filled with blood. The nurse now repeats, filling a third.

> DR. KRAMER
> You've got a short memory, kid. I don't remember that you
> were such a happy, young sick person.

Martin puts his head back in the chair and closes his eyes. We hear the echo of a scream.

FLASHBACK/1974: MARTIN'S ROOM, ISAAC'S HOUSE. NIGHT.

A close, blurry vision. A young Martin, fourteen, in bed, shivering and shaking violently, his face white and feverish, his mouth agape as he screams in agony. The room's only illumination comes from moonlight, which cuts across Martin's body.

> YOUNG MARTIN
> Dad!

YOUNG MARTIN'S POV: The door opening. A younger Isaac stands in the doorway and sees the screaming child.

CLOSE on the profile of the screaming young Martin.

BACK TO DOCTOR'S OFFICE

Dr. Kramer continues to speak.

> DR. KRAMER
> What about stress?

MARTIN

What about stress?

DR. KRAMER

Come on Martin, you avoiding stress?

MARTIN

Like family you mean?

DR. KRAMER
(smiling)

That's a factor.

MARTIN

Could you write me a note?

The nurse takes out the third tube of blood.CLOSEUP as the tubes rattle in the rack.

INT. SARAH'S APARTMENT. DAY.

Max and Sarah (in her pajamas) having a casual, unhurried breakfast: Sarah is feeding EMILY her toast. The dog goes and sits on the sofa.

SARAH

Emily, Emily, come here, come here, sit, sit down . . .

MAX

This dog needs a bath. She slept on my cashmere. I smell like mutton. And I'm seeing my wife today.

SARAH

Oh yes, we have to be careful. She might think you're dating a schnauzer.

(beat)

Sorry. That was shitty.

MAX

No. That's very good. You're getting quite good. The show could use that little edge.

The front door BUZZER sounds. Max looks questioningly.

SARAH

That's Martin.

MAX

Your brother? Martin?

SARAH

I want you to meet him . . .

Max looks startled, shakes his head, gets up and puts on his coat. Sarah watches him.

MAX

For God's sake, I can't do your family, just now, not being quite done with my own, thank you.

(he kisses her on the cheek)

Relatives right and left.

Max exits.

SARAH

(into buzzer)

Hold on, Martin.

                              MAX
                            (leaving)
See you in kiddy land.

INT. SARAH'S APARTMENT. HALLWAY. DAY.

*Max opening the door as Martin ascending the stairs smiles up, bemused.
Max squeezes wordlessly past Martin.*

                              MAX
Good morning. Just on my way.

                            MARTIN
                           (cheery)
Bye.

INT. SARAH'S APARTMENT. HALLWAY. DAY.

*POV MARTIN watching Max making a hasty exit down the stairs past
him and then at Sarah who is standing in her doorway, amused, grinning
down.*

                            MARTIN
He seems awfully nice, Sarah. You've done well.

They grin at each other and laugh.

INT. SARAH'S APT. BEDROOM AND LIVING ROOM. DAY.

*Sarah, in the bedroom, rifles through her closet, trying to come up with a
suitable costume for a meeting with her father. Martin, in the living room,*

wanders over to the mantelpiece. Pictures of the Geldharts when they were a complete family in earlier days. Sarah holds up two dresses for Martin's approval.

MARTIN

Just put on anything, anything will do. You don't have to dress for Daddy.

(beat)

You're always tracking down a daddy.

SARAH

What's that supposed to mean?

MARTIN

Just put on anything!

SARAH

(moving on)

All right. You have two choices: Anne Frank or Virgin Slut.

MARTIN

(rising)

Maybe Anne Frank was a slut.

SARAH

Martin!

MARTIN

You think she put everything in that diary?

INT. SARAH'S APARTMENT. INSERT FAMILY PICTURES. DAY.

ANGLE ON MANTELPIECE: Photos of Isaac and his wife. Isaac is formal, his wife more casual, assured and direct.

INT. SARAH'S APARTMENT. BEDROOM AND LIVING ROOM. DAY.

ANGLE ON SARAH

POV SARAH: Martin standing stock-still, staring at the family pictures, she comes up beside him and looks at them with him. He points to the picture of Isaac and their mom.

> MARTIN

Amazing, huh?

> SARAH

Yeah.

Martin replaces the photograph on the mantelpiece.

> MARTIN

To think that someone got them to stop shouting at each other for two seconds . . .

He wanders to the table and picks up the Chenard manuscript.

> MARTIN
> *(holding the manuscript)*

So what did you think of the book?

Sarah starts to put on the dress.

SARAH
(as she dresses)

Oh, I couldn't really focus. We're doing six letters back to back. Actually, you know what, it seemed funny, the dirty part, the thing with the two guys.

MARTIN

So you skimmed it? That's what you did.

SARAH

Come on, you know I don't have time to read.

MARTIN

You read magazines.

SARAH

Ha.

MARTIN

Advice on cuticles.

SARAH

What's the use?

MARTIN

How to get a guy.

SARAH

To sit down with a book. To waist your life chewing over some old story about a swan? Or that book? I mean, come on Martin, did you really read the whole book, tell me the truth, does anybody actually finish a book? I mean once they've formed an opinion of it?

MARTIN

You are the end of the world.

SARAH

So what do you call this?

She is dressed now. Martin looks at her outfit and laughs.

MARTIN

Ah. Daddy's little slut.

INT. KREEGER/GELDHART. BOARDROOM. DAY.

Louis Foukold sits at the table, eating a deli salad. Sarah and Martin sit glumly, the way one gets when someone has been talking relentlessly for longer than sixty-seven seconds.

LOUIS

So the little mouse falls in this hole. He can't get out so he's yelling Help! Help! So the elephant takes his thing and sticks it into the hole, and pops the moussie out. So the elephant says to the mouse . . .
            (he looks at Sarah)
Sarah, close your ears—no you can't hear this, so the elephant says to the mouse: If you have a big dick, you don't need a Mercedes.

There is silence.

Miss Barzakian enters, all grace—armed with a teapot on a tray. There is an exchange of glances between her and the kids as she pours tea for Louis and Martin, and carries the coffee cups over to the pot.

BARZAKIAN

Tea. Russian Caravan.

(to Martin)

I keep it for you.

MARTIN

(quietly to Barzakian)

Thank you.

*Louis grins. He knows it's a good joke. Barzakian sneaks a motherly hand
over Martin's brow—a spot check for temperature—an unspoken thing,
but caught at it, she grins.*

MARTIN

Ninety-eight point six, sunny and warm. Clear weather ahead.

LOUIS

No, there's another one.

BARZAKIAN

Okay, you two, have fun, play nice.

SARAH

Okay, we will.

LOUIS

The mouse is riding on the elephant's back—

BARZAKIAN

Louis, you want anything?

LOUIS

(as though to a bad waitress)

Yeah. A lemon would be nice.

She walks out as Isaac enters, arms raised, crossing to Sarah happily, takes in Martin, who grins.

ISAAC

Miss Barzakian, would you get me the galleys from Walter's office?
>   *(crossing to embrace Sarah with open arms)*
Sarah. Darling. Oh, you look positively grown-up.

SARAH

It's just the dress, Daddy.

ISAAC

Hmm. Like your mother.

SARAH

Oh, Daddy.

Sarah holds up Hobson-Jobson: *a thick manuscript.*

SARAH

What do you think you're doing? I mean, *Hobson-Jobson: A Glossary of Colloquial Anglo-Indian Words and Phrases?*

ISAAC

So what's the big deal? A dictionary of derivations. I think it's delightful.

They laugh.

ISAAC

Hi, Martin. So, you came too.

ANGLE ON AARON entering the room.

SARAH

So what, are we bankrupt? I'm going to walk in here and find
this place turned into Rug City?

AARON

(turns to Louis)

Louis. Would you excuse us for a minute, please?

ISAAC

Why? Why can't he stay?

Aaron gathers up Louis's things.

AARON

Because we need the room.

LOUIS

I'm not here by choice, believe me.

LOUIS

(to Isaac as Aaron leads him out)

You see what I'm saying? I need a room. You got this big room
here! You've got marketing with those children clicking on
those machines . . .

AARON

Louis, this can't be your office. People use this room.

*Aaron closes the door behind Louis. Louis can be seen looking through
the window of the boardroom.*

LOUIS

(from the outside the glass)

I just need a fucking desk!

ISAAC

Louis— I need a drink.

He walks over to the drinks cabinet. His kids are all laughing.

MARTIN

Why can't he work at home?

SARAH

Yeah. Why is he always here?

ISAAC

Would you want to be alone when you wrote that book?

Isaac opens the door of the drinks cabinet. The kids laugh; Isaac smiles.

MARTIN

So you're actually going to publish it?

There is silence for a moment.

ISAAC

Tell me Aaron, what's going on? You've been frightening everyone, Aaron?

MARTIN

No, he told us if you did, you won't be able to handle anything
on the spring list except for a couple of old reprints. Is that
right?

ISAAC

It's four volumes. He's been working on it for thirty-four years.
How can I ask him to wait? He's one of the last witnesses.

AARON

No one's saying "don't publish it," Dad, but some balance, please.

ISAAC

You know, your mother's father, started this imprint to publish serious work that was valuable to the larger world.

MARTIN

So what about Aaron's book, *Rising Tide*?

ISAAC

You read that?

AARON

I gave it to them. Both of them.

ISAAC

You have a literary opinion, Mr. Johnny-Appleseed-of-the-Hudson here?

MARTIN

Yes. I read it. I liked it. I thought it was powerful. I cried. I don't know why.

ISAAC

You're a gardener Martin, please.

SARAH

I liked it. I mean I didn't read it all, but what little I read I liked.

AARON
(to Martin)

You liked it? You really did? I thought you would. It's something, isn't it?

ISAAC

Excuse me. I don't need a little shit-ass democratic committee
here to give book reports. You think I'm going to publish some
trashy novel by a slickohipster? This book is meretricious bull-
shit! I wanted my time back after I read it.

MARTIN

I think you're misreading it.

ISAAC

I tend not to misread books.

MARTIN

You have no doubt about your own judgment.

ISAAC

Well, may I, I'll just read you a little passage here.

He picks up the manuscript from off the conference table, and says:

ISAAC
(reading)

"Alter leaned against the bar, mouth open in recollection of
those black hands on his jeans. The feeling of release and sub-
mission that comes when someone else unsnaps the buttons—
the kid's lips on him, the wetness as his shirt is lifted up toward
the spire of the Chrysler Building glowing above them, etc.,
etc., etc."

Isaac looks triumphantly at Martin.

SARAH

Well, Dad, I don't understand. What's the big deal here? I
mean, we all know about blow jobs, don't we?

ISAAC

Yes, Sarah, we know about blow jobs.

SARAH

Well then maybe you publish all those books because there's
no sex in them? They're totally flaccid. See, Dad, you just need
to get out more is all.

MARTIN

The thing is, Dad, you see, I promised Aaron that if I liked the
book, I'd support him. Whatever that meant. I like the book.
What's the big deal here?

*This takes a moment to register. Or more accurately, it registers, sinks in,
Isaac responds.*

ISAAC

What the hell is going on here? What?

AARON

I don't get it. Is this ceaseless drive to run us into the ground
circling any particular point, or is it just that in the year and a
half since Mother died, you've become suicidal?

*Isaac looks disgusted. Sarah shakes her head. Martin is expressionless.
Makes himself blank.*

ISAAC

This is simply beneath contempt, Aaron. This line of reasoning,
this, this is gutter-reasoning, kiddo, and . . .

AARON

. . . the fact remains that ever since Mom died, if we had a
graph curve it would look like the north face of Everest.

ISAAC

What? I'm destroying this company because life is not worth
living without your mother? Let me tell you something, that
wasn't exactly the greatest marriage in the world, I don't think
about her a lot these days, so phooey to that approach.
(savage)
Just stick to the numbers, Aaron!

SARAH

Who do you think you're talking about? That's my mother
you're talking about. Aaron is trying to help.

AARON

No, it's okay, it's what I signed on for. You get used to it. It's
sort of like you can insult anyone as long as it's done sort of
elegantly.

ISAAC
(surprise)
Who? Who does this? I do this? Do I really do this?

This registers with them.

AARON

Dad. Do you remember when we had a bestseller? It was six
years ago. Can't you just simply trust me? Once? Just on this.

There is a moment. Silence.

ISAAC

No.

*Martin sighs. Nobody speaks. When Martin does, it is with a quiet ex-
hausted calm.*

MARTIN

All right, then I'll sign my shares of this company over to Aaron. That would make him the majority stockholder.

There is a silence.

SARAH

What? Martin, hold on, what are you doing? Come on. Are you kidding here? I didn't agree to this.

Another silence.

SARAH

Martin! We're not like this. Are we like this? Over money? You have got to find some way to compromise. All of you. Because this is just horseshit.

ISAAC

Well, I sense that your little sister would not be in with you on this takeover. So. Sarah. Darling.

AARON

There's no way, Dad, there's no way you can win this one.

SARAH

Hold it. Why don't you bother asking me? Nobody bothers asking me what I think. Look, I don't want to turn this into some horrible little thing, all right, but Martin, if you hand your shares to Aaron, then I'm going to hand mine over to Dad.

AARON

Sarah.

SARAH

Well, I'm sorry, nobody bothers asking me!

MARTIN

Sarah! Don't.

AARON

Sarah, what are you doing?

Martin is sitting still. He is taking it all in, expressionless.

AARON

Sarah. There's no cash. We're on empty here.

SARAH

Come on, one of you, bend a little.

AARON

Bend. It's way beyond that. He just got you to offer him your stock. He'll have fifty-five percent of this house. That's just what he's after.

SARAH

I'm sorry, Aaron.

AARON
(acid)

Well, I guess I'll just have to find some way to think of this as a "positive."

ISAAC

No you don't. My son.

(beat)

47

You are fired. I will give you a week to clear your desk. I will give you letters of recommendation. But I will not speak with you. I will not communicate with you. I will not give at all. Kiddo. To the victor go the spoils.

ANGLE ON *Sarah, taking it in and figuring it out.*

SARAH

Oh. I get it. I get it.
                    (*she hits herself; to Aaron*)
I'm so stupid.
                    (*back to Isaac*)
You want to use me to screw Aaron, and you think I'll go along with that?

ISAAC

Sarah . . .

SARAH
(*gathering pages*)
No, no. You think that you can fire us? Look, I'm sorry, I'm going to give my shares to Aaron because you don't understand. You don't know how to love.

And silence. Nobody dares look at anyone for a moment. When anyone speaks, of course it is Aaron.

AARON

Let's be clear about this: You just handed me control of this company.

SARAH

Yes. I did.

There is silence.

AARON
(to Isaac)

You did this to yourself. It didn't have to happen. You knew
this was coming. You want to hate me? Go ahead. Hate me. I
have no choice.

ISAAC

You understand, Aaron, sweetheart, you'll just be part of the
big carcinogenic pile of trash.

AARON
(rises to his feet)

Well, then all I can do is sift through it.

Aaron starts to walk out the door.

ISAAC
(as Aaron exits)

Aaron.
(beat)

I hope it works out for you.

*Aaron leaves. Martin and Sarah don't move. Isaac walks up the stairs to
his office.*

SARAH
(rising to her feet)

Look, I've got a show. I have a show. I have . . . Dad . . .
(to Martin)

Bye.

*Isaac looks at her indifferently, and continues up the stairs. Sarah leaves.
Martin sits and waits.*

FADE TO:

INT. MUSSELBLAT'S LAW OFFICE. DAY.

Isaac's lawyer MUSSELBLAT's office. It's Isaac, (excited and scrubbed, new suit,etc.,dressed for a brawl, and his eyes gleaming,) Musselblat, on one side, (a slob), and a tense AARON and his lawyer, COX, on the other. COX is an old pro, not a guy who goes for a fight when a scotch and soda will be just as effective in solving the problem.

                              COX
And certain predetermined assets assigned to the new corpora-
tion formed by Mr. Isaac Geldhart . . .

                         MUSSELBLAT
What Mr. Geldhart wants is his name.

                              COX
Removed from Kreeger/Geldhart Publishers?

                         MUSSELBLAT
He proposes that the company that Aaron runs be Kreeger.
Kreeger Books.

                             ISAAC
Yes. Kreeger. Go back to the original name.

                             AARON
Dad, this is just revenge.

                              COX
                            (slow)
Mr. Geldhart. You need to be reminded that your children

share your name and that you are still a major stockholder in this company.

> ISAAC
> *(relishing this, turns to Aaron)*
Not for long, kiddo.

Isaac smiles widely at Aaron. He looks alive, happy in his very well-cut suit. For he is at war.

INT. KREEGER/GELDHART PUBLISHERS. ELEVATOR BANK. DAY.

Sarah getting off the elevator. A new logo in raised letters is being affixed to the office wall: KREEGER BOOKS. Sarah takes this in and continues on.

INT. KREEGER/GELDHART PUBLISHERS. HALLWAY/FOYER. DAY.

ANGLE ON SARAH: A young man is now working at Miss Barzakian's desk. The OTANIS have moved in. There is a quiet string of Japanese whispering. Sarah sees the Otanis, who are projecting pie charts in the boardroom.

ANGLE ON SARAH walking past the YOUNG FEY RECEPTIONIST.

> RECEPTIONIST
> *(rising, as Aaron appears)*
You're Sarah, aren't you? She who talks to the animals. I'm Trevor.

> SARAH
Hi.

RECEPTIONIST

Aaron's right in there.

Sarah continues toward Aaron's office.

INT. KREEGER/GELDHART PUBLISHERS. AARON'S OFFICE. DAY.

Sarah enters Aaron's office. Aaron sits at his desk. Val stands opposite him.

SARAH

What is this? What is happening here?

AARON

I know, I know. This is what he wanted.

VAL

You want some coffee?

SARAH

No, thank you.

AARON

This is Val.

SARAH

Oh, hi. Nice work.

She gestures to the manuscript.

VAL
(shy)
Oh, not much there, but . . . you're funny with the kids.

An awkward moment. Val leaves.

AARON

He's going to be fine. He took the Japanese for a couple mil.

SARAH

He's not fine.

AARON

Have you talked to him?

SARAH

He hangs up on me. He's not fine.
>   *(gesturing down the hall toward Val)*
He's cute, if you like boys.

AARON

Sarah, the man is having fun.

INT. OFFICE OF GELDHART PUBLISHING. DAY.

The warehouse district. Downtown. A loftlike space. Miss Barzakian at a desk. She is trying to arrange it, to make the best of diminished circumstances. Though certainly a large step down from Kreeger/Geldhart, one understands why Isaac would have chosen this space. It is airy and light and possessed of a certain industrial sophistication. Offscreen the voice of Louis Foukold raised in rage.

LOUIS

You don't sneak it up on me in the middle of the night like a fucking thief. Fucking idiot. That's it. That's it. Moronic subliterate bastard—

Isaac closes the door behind Louis. Louis looks at Barzakian through his rage. He sits near her desk.

BARZAKIAN

Louis, Louis, just a minute. *(beat)* You might consider going a
little easier on Mr. Geldhart. Louis. He's been very loyal to
you, wouldn't you say that's true?

*Louis slumps visibly. He looks so tired. Isaac peers out of his office, looks
down at Barzakian.*

BARZAKIAN

How about some tea?

ISAAC

Luis, come with me.

LOUIS

Now what?

Louis follows Barzakian and Isaac.

INT. GELDHART PUBLISHING, WORKROOM. DAY.

*Otto and the printer from the earlier scene. Also, a BINDER. Miss Bar-
zakian takes notes as Isaac confers on binding. Louis hovers about. On
the table is the proposed book; the binding, the paper, etc. There are three
or four different choices of leather bindings at hand.*

ISAAC
(to Otto the printer)

You can do it?

OTTO

Of course we can do it. Can you pay for it? It'll take five guys
three months to sew bindings by hand.

ISAAC

Well, it should. It's not an easy job.

OTTO

Ever hear of the Industrial Revolution?

ISAAC

We know what looks best though, don't we Otto? And we
know what will last.

Isaac walks away. Louis follows, then Barzakian.

LOUIS
(in background)
Why? Why can't a machine do it?

ISAAC

What do you know about it?

BARZAKIAN

Get us a realistic figure on the binding, Otto.

*Under the above, we see and hear in background, Isaac and Louis bick-
ering.*

ISAAC
(background)
Please, Louis, just let me do my publishing.

OTTO

Will someone tell him it's just a book.

INT. ISAAC'S HOUSE. LIVING ROOM. DAY.

Miss Barzakian on a library ladder. Floor to ceiling books. Isaac sits at a desk looking through his collection of illustrated letters.

ISAAC

Ever see this Thackeray? What a thing . . . to be a friend of Thackeray's. He bombarded his friends with letters. Little drawings he did. You ever see this?

BARZAKIAN
(gestures to a red-spined book)
You know the spine is loose on *David Copperfield*.

ISAAC
(instantly annoyed)
Well don't pull it! You'll only make it worse.

The phone rings. Isaac ignores it, glaring at Barzakian.

BARZAKIAN

I'm not pulling it.

ISAAC

That's signed by Dickens.

The phone continues to ring. Isaac is oblivious.

ISAAC

Do you know who that set belonged to?

BARZAKIAN

Jack London.

Isaac is stopped momentarily as he realizes Barzakian knows his collection better than he does.

ISAAC
(ineffectually)
Right, so don't pull it.

The ANSWERING MACHINE CLICKS ON. Martin's voice.

MARTIN
(on machine)
Dad. It's Martin again.

Barzakian looks at Isaac. He goes back to his illustrated letters.

MARTIN
I hear things are going great. Uh. I can't tell you how happy
that makes me. I saw a thing in the *Times* about the new company.

Isaac crosses to the phone, lifts the handle, slams it down, and disconnects
the call.

ISAAC
Well. This one you never saw. This cost plenty. I never even
told Rena I bought this.

BARZAKIAN
(back at the shelf, takes out a first edition)
What's Twain doing with Dickens?

ISAAC
Oh. *Huck Finn*! Sarah's copy for her seventh birthday!

Barzakian descends the ladder with the Twain.

ISAAC

She completely fell in love with Huck. He broke her heart. Tell me, Miss Barzakian. Do you think girls are more empathetic than boys?

She looks at him. He continues.

ISAAC

Well, I mean, not *you*. But girls. When I took her to Pinocchio, she was what? She was four—she yelled at the whale, "Don't eat that boy."
        (mumbles almost to himself)
"Don't eat that boy."

Barzakian holds out the book for Isaac.

BARZAKIAN

She should have this.

Isaac does not move. She sets the book on the desk.

INT. GELDHART PUBLISHING. RECEPTION. DAY.

Sarah walks into the reception area. Barzakian gets up from her desk. Sarah holds a flowering plant and an ABC Carpet bag. Isaac's raised voice can be heard in the background.

BARZAKIAN

This is it, you are in the right place.

SARAH

(taking in the spartan place)
Well. Industrial chic. I'm too early . . . I'm a little early.

BARZAKIAN

No, it's fine.

SARAH

Here. This is for you.

She pulls out an ornate pillow from the ABC Carpet bag. It has an embroidered unicorn tapestry on it. She cringes slightly, apologetic. Perhaps the wrong choice. Barzakian smiles.

BARZAKIAN

(Barzakian takes the Mark Twain from a drawer and slips it unseen by Sarah into a pile of documents)
We haven't settled here, it's just transitional really.

SARAH

(cringing)
I thought you might have a little sofa. Ah, back in stride is he?

Sarah places the pillow on an undistinguished bench.

BARZAKIAN

(holding the pile of papers hiding the book)
I'll get him.

SARAH

(picking something up in her tone)
Are you sure about this?

BARZAKIAN

Don't worry.

Sarah sits in the undistinguished bench, the pillow at her side, unicorn facing out. She looks at it critically, and turns it around to its blank velvet side.

INT. GELDHART PUBLISHING. ISAAC'S OFFICE. DAY.

Barzakian waiting for Isaac to get off the phone. She stands holding her documents and the book.

> ISAAC
> *(on phone)*
> No, I don't know which account you're talking about but I will give you Miss Barzakian. Yes, the one who does the billing questions . . .

Looks up to Barzakian, helpless, mimes her taking the phone. He gives the phone to Barzakian. Sighs and gestures helplessly.

> BARZAKIAN
> *(into phone)*
> Yes? Yes?

> ISAAC
> There's a bank, now it's called another bank, and I don't even know the name of the first bank . . . and now they want forms . . . "W" forms . . .

> BARZAKIAN
> I'll take care of it. She's outside. (She displays Sarah's copy of *Huckleberry Finn*.)
> *(into phone)*
> Yes. Two different companies. This is Geldhart. You want Kreeger.

She sets the Mark Twain book down in front of him. He stares at it.

INT. GELDHART PUBLISHING. ISAAC'S OFFICE. DAY.

ANGLE ON ISAAC: *Getting up from his desk and walking to the door. Sees Sarah sitting in reception.*

INT. GELDHART PUBLISHING. RECEPTION. DAY.

Sarah stands as soon as she sees him.

ANGLE ON ISAAC *grabbing a passing worker, a burly CUBAN man, Miquel.*

ISAAC

(pulling the man with him)

Miquel, there's a woman making some trouble out there.

Then he pulls Miquel into the reception area. Barzakian sees this and rushes out of the office.

INT. GELDHART PUBLISHING. RECEPTION. DAY.

ISAAC

(to Miquel)

Remove her please.

Isaac goes back into his office and closes the door. Sarah looks to Barzakian.

BARZAKIAN
(quickly)
Miquel, it's okay. She will . . . Sarah, Sarah . . .

Miquel moves to escort Sarah out. Sarah pulls away and storms out. Barzakian follows her outside.

EXT. GELDHART PUBLISHING. DAY.

Barzakian follows an enraged Sarah into the street.

BARZAKIAN
Sarah! I'm sorry, Sarah, I did this wrong.

SARAH
No, no. It's not your fault. He's a hateful prick. He set me up.
I'm not doing this anymore.

She walks away to get a taxi. Barzakian watches, helpless.

INT. SARAH'S APARTMENT. DINING ROOM. NIGHT.

A little dinner party. Max, Sarah, and Martin. Max displays all the reluctance of a (married) man going deeper than he thought or cared to go. Some nice Preservation Hall band quietly playing. But it's not helping.

SARAH
This can't be right, it's not happening. This gnocchi isn't coming up. Where is it? It's supposed to float up. It's like they went to, to Atlantis or something.

MARTIN

Sarah, let me give you a hand.

SARAH

I'm fine, I'm fine, I'm fine. Shit!

MARTIN

Have you always been in children's television?

MAX

BBC first, actually, I came over with *Alphabet Park*, which we
first did there, Funny squirrels with jumpers and brollies, was
my err . . . creation.

Martin doesn't know what to say.

MARTIN
(*smiling enthusiastically*)

Squirrels with jumpers?

MAX
(*serious*)

Clicky the Squirrel.
(*beat, he smiles in apology*)

Kids loved it.

Max shrugs. Toys with his salad. He lifts a flower.

MAX

Is this a petunia, love?

MARTIN
(*looks at it quickly*)

Nasturtium.

INT. SARAH'S APARTMENT. KITCHEN. NIGHT.

A catastrophe. The kind that happens when someone has gone over their head, as has Sarah, in trying to make everything perfect, her reach of The Rules of Cooking *has exceeded her grasp. Sarah stands at the stove, panicking over some boiling gnocchi.*

INT. SARAH'S APARTMENT. DINING ROOM. NIGHT.

ANGLE ON DINNER TABLE: Max and Martin uncomfortable together. Both struggle with busy colorful, demanding salads.

> SARAH
> *(in kitchen—regarding the gnocchi)*
I see them!

> MAX
I think it's not unlike what you do; teaching. You get to nurture, do exactly as you please—

> MARTIN
Yeah, from time to time. Mostly it's refereeing crying jags.

> SARAH
Martin is a wonderful teacher.

> MARTIN
Sarah is one of my most devoted students.

> SARAH
Martin.

MARTIN

You've seen the African violet by the bed? The one with the grey ashen pallor?

MARTIN AND MAX'S POV; SARAH IN KITCHEN

She inexpertly tries to pick up one of the gnocchi; it burns her hand and she drops it on the floor, where it lays like a stone. She fishes out another one with a spoon. Tastes it. Spits it into the sink.

SARAH

These taste like little balls of raw flour.

She dumps the gnocchi in the trash.

MAX

It's only a meal, darling.

SARAH
(looking at the trash)
None of this does what they say that it's going to do. It just doesn't.

MAX

She's hyperexcited.

SARAH
(defeated—comes into dining room)
The roast is done.

MAX

You don't really even have to direct her. She knows when she's wrong. Great instincts.

Sarah glares at Max. She exits, closing sliding door to bedroom. Max and Martin say nothing for a moment.

MARTIN

You want to go bowling?

INT. BOWLING ALLEY. NIGHT.

Sarah and Martin, clearly first-time bowlers, having a hell of a good time.

ANGLE ON THE BOWLING ALLEY BAR: Max sits, deeply embarrassed, drinking steadily, not looking at the spectacle of Sarah and Martin's bowling show. YOUNG NYU STUDENTS, and a FAMILY, populate a few of the other lanes.

INT. BOWLING ALLEY. NIGHT.

ANGLE ON SARAH BOWLING: She slams her bowling ball into the family's lane, knocking several pins over. She and Martin collapse in gales of hilarity.

ANGLE ON MAX getting drunk in the background as Sarah and Martin have an extremely good time.

INT. GELDHART PUBLISHING. DAY.

Expensive looking volumes being tossed to the floor. Volume one of the Foukold Nazi medical experiments book.

ISAAC

You see?

ANGLE ON ISAAC kneeling, cutting pages with an X-ACTO knife and hurling them down to the floor. There is a palette full of boxes filled with books. One of the boxes has been opened and several books removed. The staff, including Barzakian and Miquel, watch helplessly.

ANGLE ON ISAAC

Stops cutting, spent. He hands the X-ACTO knife to an assistant.

> ISAAC
>
> Cut them all. Every last one.

Otto blocks the assistant's path.

> OTTO
> *(furious)*
> You're being crazy! What's the matter with you?

Isaac looks ferociously disgusted.

> OTTO
> *(angrier still)*
> This is beautiful work!

Isaac grabs the book from out of Otto's hands and rips out a page. Otto gasps. Isaac hands it back to Otto.

> ISAAC
> You call this beautiful? This paper, this is *Time* magazine! How could this have happened? Who? Who is responsible for this?

There is silence. Nobody looks anywhere. Isaac is red-faced.

BARZAKIAN
(after another silence)

It costs over two hundred dollars to make that book. Just one book. That book. You know how much it would have cost to make the book you wanted?

Isaac is breathing heavily. He turns to the assistant.

ISAAC

We start over.

Isaac turns to leave.

ISAAC

Cut every last one.

The assistants do nothing.

ISAAC
(stops, walking out)

Cut them!

Miss Barzakian turns away as the assistant begins the awesome task.

INT. GELDHART PUBLISHING. RECEPTION/OFFICE. NIGHT.

Miss Barzakian is cleaning out her desk. Isaac walks up to her, carrying an envelope. He turns on her desk light. He looks at a postcard, which he holds in his hands.

ISAAC

Wait till you see what I got.

Barzakian continues to pack. He looks at a war-torn landscape on card-board, with some spidery writing on it.

ISAAC

This is from Singleton, the dealer, you know Singleton, we got the *Coleridge* from him last year. Well, I mean he had no idea what he had, it was a steal. Seventy-five thousand dollars. Don't worry . . . it was a trade. The first edition *Ulysses* and ten thousand in cash. This is a postcard painted by Adolf Hitler when he was a student. He bought his art supplies from a Jew. Who thought he had talent. And gave him, just gave him his materials. He was not without a certain basic rudimentary tal-ent, was he not? You would certainly hope that he would be utterly devoid of talent, I mean, it would have shed some tiny glimmer of light on all the subsequent years, on all that came after. But no . . . this is no slur of muddy noncolor. There is something here, yes?

BARZAKIAN

I suppose. *(Pause)* There's a man coming to fix the leak, and I left the number of the bookkeeper I hired.

Miss Barzakian leaves the room with her box. Isaac doesn't even look up.

INT. BOOK BINDERY. DAY.

Isaac examining the finished Foukold book. The binder looks on. Isaac's hands glide across a page. He murmurs his appreciation. LOUIS watches. He sees the book for the first time. He's afraid to ask.

LOUIS

Have we got what we are after?

                              ISAAC
  We do.

*Louis looks thrilled. He takes the book in his hands. He starts to examine
it.*

Isaac watches gingerly before gently wrestling it away from the old man.

*ANGLE ON ISAAC: Handing the book to the binder. Louis looks on,
perplexed.*

                              LOUIS
  Where is he going?

He starts after binder.

                              ISAAC
  Louis, I have to tell you something. He's going to keep them
  for a while.

Louis looks nonplussed.

                              LOUIS
  Why?

Isaac doesn't answer for a moment.

                              ISAAC
  I have to pay him something first.

                              LOUIS
                           (incredulous)
  You didn't pay him?

ISAAC
(defensive)
Louis, I'm going to pay him.

The binder returns. Louis doesn't know what to say or do.

BINDER
You know where to find them when you raise their bail.

ISAAC
(turning to binder, as he passes)
Some of that stitching is a bit casual.

BINDER
(not stopping)
Then when you pay for them you can destroy them.

INT. MC CORMACK BOOKSELLERS. DAY.

An extremely fastidious MIDDLE-AGED MAN checks carefully through Isaac's Dickens set. Isaac sits impatiently nearby.

ISAAC
I was going to go to Sotheby's but, well, they take forever there.

The man waves over a SECOND BOOK-DEALER, an older gentleman in his shirtsleeves. The older man looks on as the younger dealer picks his way through Little Dorrit.

OLDER DEALER
Oh, yes. I remember these. Your wife.

                              ISAAC

Yes.

                           OLDER DEALER

She came in every day for a month before she bought them.

                              ISAAC

Jack London, you know.

                           OLDER DEALER

She came in so often, I thought she had a thing for me. But she
was only frightened of spending so much money.

                          YOUNGER DEALER

The spine is loose on this *Copperfield*.

The older dealer watches Isaac.

                           OLDER DEALER

Then don't touch it. How much?

                              ISAAC

Twelve thousand.

                           OLDER DEALER

Your wife got a good deal.

EXT. GELDHART PUBLISHING. DAY.

*An office-furniture company truck backed up to the open loading door.
Desks and chairs being removed from the office and put into the truck.
A lot of background NOISE AND TRAFFIC—a busy time of day.*

EXT. GELDHART PUBLISHING. DAY.

Late afternoon. Silent streets. The truck is gone. Loading door closed.

INT. GELDHART PUBLISHING. DAY.

The now empty warehouse. Isaac pacing nervously. A truck pulls up.

ANGLE ON ISAAC as he walks quickly to the truck, steps in and prys open a crate. Carefully packed away copies of volume one of The Science of Genocide: The Doctors of the Holocaust *by Louis Foukold. Isaac carefully lifts up a book, examining it.*

CUT TO ISAAC

He is ecstatic.

> TRUCK DRIVER
> Those belong to you?

> ISAAC
> All good things to those who wait.

EXT. RIZZOLI BOOKSELLERS. 57TH STREET. DAY.

Isaac and Louis entering. Isaac carries the four volume set of The Science of Genocide: The Doctors of the Holocaust. *They pass the display window with its picture of Val Chenard.*

ANGLE ON WINDOW FROM ISAAC'S POV: A pile of VAL CHENARD'S book, Rising Tide, *displayed prominently.*

INT. RIZZOLI BOOKSELLERS. DAY.

Isaac and Louis cross the main room and head for stairs to the office. Louis stops at a pile of Rising Tide.

ANGLE ON ISAAC stopping on stairs to wait for Louis.

ANGLE ON LOUIS examining, with some interest, a copy of Rising Tide. *Val Chenard's face smiling sheepishly up from the back cover. Louis peers at it, reading carefully.*

> LOUIS
> *(peering at the posterboard, on which there is a critic's quote)*
> "A glitteringly black sexual truffle of Swiftian ambition."
> *(looks up at Isaac)*

> ISAAC
> Louis!

He looks closely at a little black sticker on the book. Isaac waits impatiently on the stairs.

> LOUIS
> *(clearly impressed, loud)*
> "Soon to be a Mike Nichols."
> *(beat, looks up at Isaac)*
> Who's Mike Nichols?

Isaac continues up the steps.

INT. RIZZOLI BOOKSELLERS. BUYER'S OFFICE. DAY.

She is young, pleasant, and intelligent. She looks over the Foukold book as Isaac and Louis sit attentively by. After a significant silence, Isaac speaks.

ISAAC

Mr. Berlusconti felt that it sounded quite interesting. But that you would be the one to make the decision about the quantity and whatever else.

BUYER

My God, this is awful. I mean, it's beautiful . . . work. But it's very difficult.

ISAAC

Well, yes. It's not an easy read. No.

BUYER

(turning the book over in her hands)
But how magnificently made! Congratulations.

ISAAC

Thank you.

BUYER

Not for us though, Mr. Geldhart. It's much too expensive. We couldn't sell it. We couldn't even buy it.

LOUIS

It's an important subject. It's never been adequately chronicled.

BUYER

Of course.

LOUIS

Only in magazines. There is only fact here. No conjecture. It took a long time.

ISAAC

Louis. She doesn't want it.

The buyer picks up the phone.

BUYER
(on phone)

Angela?

ISAAC
(to Louis)

You ready?

BUYER
(on phone)

Yes, do we have any extra copies of *The World of Moorish Tiles*? Good. Could you see that Mr. Geldhardt gets a copy, he's on his way down now. Thank you.

EXT. EAST RIVER PARK. DAY.

Isaac and Louis on a bench. The books between them. Louis feeding bits of pretzel to the pigeons, first carefully wiping off the mustard. Isaac is sort of adrift. Pigeons flap about. A cold wind blows off the East River.

ANGLE ON LOUIS wiping mustard off the pretzel.

ISAAC

Why do you get mustard if you're just going to scrape it off?

LOUIS
(tossing)

They put it on, I didn't ask.

ISAAC

Well, you shouldn't use mustard, you shouldn't use salt . . .
sodium . . . hypertension . . . blood pressure . . .

LOUIS

(spilling mustard on his sleeve)

Shit.

As Isaac speaks, they both notice mustard on Louis's sleeve. Louis wipes
it off, revealing the pale blue-green tatoo of a concentration camp survivor.

ISAAC

(beat; points to Louis's tatoo)

One gets covetous sometimes. Little badge of honor there.

Louis nods and continues feeding the pigeons.

ISAAC

My mother must have had one. My sister. My father. Brother.

(beat)

Louis continues to feed pigeons.

Well, oh, I never say anything about this. You know.
Why talk? Why bother? I wasn't in the camps. I was happily
eating smoked eel in the attic with my Alexander Dumas. What
did I know? I was sheltered, protected by my cousins. And then
I got out of the attic and into the wrecked world.

He looks around at the park.

LOUIS

(handing Isaac a pretzel)

You want to give them something?

HOLD ON ISAAC AND LOUIS FEEDING THE PIGEONS.

EXT. ISAAC'S APARTMENT. DAY.

Sarah, Martin, and Aaron nervously waiting outside the doorway.

ANGLE ON MARTIN dressed far too warm for the weather as if fighting off a fever.

EXT. ISAAC'S APARTMENT. DAY.

ANGLE ON MISS BARZAKIAN DISEMBARKING FROM A CAB: They watch as Miss Barzakian gets out of a cab to join them. Miss Barzakian uses her keys and they go inside.

INT. ISAAC'S APT. DOWNSTAIRS HALLWAY/LANDING. DAY

Miss Barzakian opening his door.

ANGLE FROM UPSTAIRS HALLWAY: Barzakian, Martin, Sarah, and Aaron walking up the stairs. A sense of foreboding—something is terribly wrong. Camera follows them up into the room. Their expressions are of varying degrees of disbelief.

INT. ISAAC'S HOUSE. LIVING ROOM. DAY.

LONG SHOT OF MARTIN, SARAH, AND AARON IN MIDDLE OF ROOM

Barzakian in the doorway, all of them taking it all in. Filthy dishes scattered about the floor and on tables, piles and piles of newspapers, manuscripts, unopened mail. An atmosphere of unhealthy decay and neglect permeates the place. Along the interior wall are unopened crates of the Foukold book. Stacked to the ceiling. The bookcase wall is startlingly bare; a few random books lie on their sides here and there.

SARAH

Oh, my God. All those years he asked us to clean up our rooms.

AARON

It's Miss Haversham's house.

BARZAKIAN

Yes, I came to drop off my keys. I tried to contact him for months, but he never returned my calls.

SARAH

Join the club.

AARON

So is anyone going to say what we're all thinking here?

MARTIN

No, why don't you tell us what we're all thinking, Aaron.

AARON

He can't take care of himself.

Nobody says anything.

AARON

Someone is going to have to start making decisions for him.
We're not helpless here. There are things we can do.

SARAH

What?

AARON

We can have him declared incompetent by the courts.

Aaron is opening up bills, collection notices. Sarah shakes her head.

What, Sarah, talk to me.

SARAH

This is not a legal problem, Aaron. This is a medical problem.
He needs to see a doctor.

AARON

Well that's fine, Sarah, but who's going to look after him, *you*?

SARAH

No. No. I can't do it, Aaron.

MARTIN
(emphatic)
I'll do it. No courts. None of that.

SARAH

Martin—

She gestures. "You can't afford to do this . . ."

MARTIN

He just needs a little attention is all.

AARON

He's not going to let you near him.

Nobody says anything. Sarah shakes her head. "Impossible. Attention?"

ANGLE ON MARTIN *looking around the room at the monumental task before him.*

INT. LONG SHOT KITCHEN FROM HALLWAY. NIGHT.

Martin in the kitchen engaged in the Sisyphean task of cleaning up. He exits the kitchen. We follow him into the living room, which is now markedly cleaner than before. He continues his work there.

INT. ISAAC'S APARTMENT. NIGHT.

Martin walking downstairs in the empty house. He goes into his old bedroom.

INT. MARTIN'S OLD BEDROOM. NIGHT.

The room is as he left it fifteen years ago: floor to ceiling books everywhere. A window looks out on a small urban garden, now overgrown. A single bed (surrounded by bookcases, improvised during his student years), a lamp, a desk.

ANGLE ON MARTIN *taking it all in.*

INT. MARTIN'S BEDROOM. LATER. MOONLIGHT.

Martin lies on the bed in the darkness, in the near dark, coughing. We hear KEYS turning in lock.

ANGLE ON MARTIN lying on the bed, anticipating arrival of Isaac.

INT. ISAAC'S HOUSE. HALLWAY/MARTIN'S BEDROOM. NIGHT.

ANGLE ON ISAAC opening the front door, light floods in from the hall-way. He is about to close the door. Martin coughs. Isaac stops.

> ISAAC
>
> Martin? Martin? Is that *you*?

He closes the door, moves to the bedroom. Martin is now dimly visible.

> ISAAC
>
> How did you get in?

> MARTIN
>
> Barzakian.

ANGLE ON ISAAC; MARTIN'S POV

> ISAAC
> *(vague)*
>
> Oh, Barzakian. She turned on me, you know. I was going to
> change the lock but I forgot.

Isaac starts to walk upstairs.

> ISAAC
> *(abstracted)*
>
> There's some split pea in the freezer. I forgot to put the top on,
> so it might be a little frosty, but . . .

He resumes his climb up the stairs. Martin sits, unmoving.

EXT. MARTIN'S HOUSE. UPSTATE. DAY.

Sarah and Martin root beneath a tree for mushrooms. From within the house we hear Brazilian jazz.

                    SARAH
Martin, I'm getting filthy.

                    MARTIN
Stop whining.

                    AARON
                (in background)
Val! Door!

                    MARTIN
Three leaves is poison ivy, so be careful.

                    SARAH
Where? What?

                    MARTIN
No. Relax. You're fine. Come on, help me.

                    SARAH
I'm not dressed for this. I don't have my hunting and gathering clothes.

                    MARTIN
                (imploring)
We'll have some nice mushrooms.

SARAH
(searching the ground halfheartedly)
They have nice mushrooms at the supermarket. Oh! Here's one! Look.

She reaches down and picks it from the ground. Martin winces.

MARTIN
Well that one's . . . poisonous.

Sarah, horrified, drops the mushroom.

MARTIN
(calmly still searching for mushrooms)
Don't touch your mouth or eyes or anything, you'll blow up like a puffer fish.

SARAH
(standing paralyzed)
How can you live like this?

MARTIN
Are your fingers numb yet?

INT. MARTIN'S HOUSE. KITCHEN. EVENING.

Martin walks into the kitchen, hands overflowing with mushrooms, which he hands to Val.

MARTIN
Look at this, look at these beauties!

VAL

Oh God, we have to eat these?

SARAH

(at sink, washing hands ferociously)

Hey. Back off. I'm toxic. Is there a center for poison control?

MARTIN

Sarah, Sarah, I was joking.

Val, overcome by the Brazilian rhythms, pulls Aaron into an improvised samba. Martin edges around them to Sarah.

INT. MARTIN'S HOUSE. NIGHT.

Aaron, Val, and Sarah sit at the table with Martin, who has a little pile of wrapped birthday presents in front of him. Sarah is methodically eating her cake around the still intact lit candle. There is a moody silence.

SARAH

Look, do whatever you want but don't expect me to contribute. I thought I was coming here for your birthday party.

VAL

(indicates a present)

Open mine first.

AARON

(as Martin picks up the present)

Martin, you know this sounds crazy.

MARTIN

Yeah?

AARON

You want me to buy two hundred and fifty thousand dollars
worth of—

MARTIN

(overlapping)

Two hundred and thirty-six thousand.

AARON

Whatever. Of his little how-to-atrocity handbook, after what
he did to the company?

MARTIN

You made ten times that on Val's book.

VAL

(to Aaron)

You did?

AARON

Martin, that wasn't profit.

MARTIN

Oh?

Sarah looks at Aaron.

AARON

(as Sarah mocks him)

Shut up! We had marketing costs and—

VAL

(to Aaron)

You've got the money. You've got it.

Aaron turns to Martin, defeated. A gesture of "You win."

AARON

All right. I'll do it. Happy birthday, Martin.

SARAH

(to Aaron)

Why would Dad accept money from you?

Aaron looks to Martin, who has engaged himself in the unwrapping of Val's present. He extracts a FLYING NUN LUNCH PAIL.

MARTIN

(utterly bewildered)

Oh. Well. Excellent. It's ah . . . I don't have this one.

Val smiles winningly at Martin.

INT. MARTIN'S HOUSE. LIVING ROOM. NIGHT.

Martin carries blankets to Aaron and Val, who have turned the sofa into a bed and are in their underwear.

AARON

What time do you want to get up?

VAL

I don't have to get up, you do.

AARON

Oh, that's right, I forgot. I'm the one that works.

Martin hands Aaron the blankets.

Yeah, thanks, just in case.

MARTIN

Ah, thanks for a great birthday.

AARON

Yeah, it was fun. Thanks for having us up.

MARTIN
(awkward and eager to split)
Yeah, okay. Good night.

AARON

Good night.

VAL

Good night, Martin.

MARTIN

Good night.

INT. MARTIN'S HOUSE. BEDROOM. NIGHT.

ANGLE ON MARTIN *retreating into his bedroom. Martin lies down on a sleeping bag on the floor, perpendicular to the foot of his single bed. Sarah, in the single bed, pivots to talk to Martin.*

ANGLE ON SARAH *scrambling around to peek down at Martin.*

SARAH

You awake?

Offscreen, we hear Aaron and Val laughing.

> SARAH
> *(under Aaron's offscreen laughter)*
> Nice to see him happy finally.

> MARTIN
> Yeah. How 'bout you? How 'bout you and Lord Maximilian.

> SARAH
> Well, chronologically speaking, we still can't agree as to who dumped who. What about you, you having any kind of a life up here? Is there somebody in your life?
> *(pause)*
> Do you have somebody?

> MARTIN
> What a thought.

> SARAH
> I was just wondering.

> MARTIN
> I don't think this family's made for breeding.

Sarah scoots back to the right side of the bed.

> SARAH
> You have no faith.

INT. ISAAC'S APT. LIVING ROOM. DAY.

Louis stands behind Issac, who looks at a letter.

ANGLE ON LETTER IN ISAAC'S HANDS

The letterhead reads Iophon Press.

ISAAC

Io-Io-Phon. Iophon.
(to Martin as he enters)
Martin, I never heard of these publishers.

MARTIN
(his back to them, casual, vague)
Iophon Press. It's a half dozen university presses here, and some
European partners dividing the risk on you know, important
projects . . .
(thinks)
. . . and some foundations, with a focus on medicine.

ISAAC
(triumphant to Louis)
Bingo! I told you! The universities! The foundations! We were
wasting our time in the marketplace.

*Isaac, in his excitement at his victory snorts derisively at Louis. Martin is
now staring at him.*

ISAAC

You, you had to be such a snob.
(turns to Martin)
He thinks the universities are run by Farrakhan. So. Okay.
Iophon. Now, Martin, you want to know the lesson? You don't
back down. But you, you wouldn't understand that; in your
tree house, dropping your little spores on the wind. You see the
lesson?

MARTIN
(exhausted)

Yeah, I see it.

ISAAC

You know, you think it's all over, you think it's all finished and
then there's this guy. Iophon.
(beat)
Actually, I think I got a letter from them, I didn't even answer
him.

MARTIN
(no big deal, but really holding his breath)

Yeah, well, they're smart, they know that you couldn't sell it,
so they're looking to buy it cheap . . .

He gestures to the crates. Isaac looks suspicious.

ISAAC

What exactly is cheap?

MARTIN

Two-thirty-six.

ISAAC

Two-thirty-six what?

MARTIN

Two hundred and thirty six thousand.

ISAAC

That is an absurd, ridiculous figure.
(beat; Isaac thinks)

So okay. Now. We're back in the business. We counter. Two and a half million.

MARTIN
(overlapping)

No, no, no. We don't counter, Dad. This is a take it or leave it offer. There's no room for that.

ISAAC
(shrugs again)

Then we leave it.

MARTIN
(overlapping)

No, we don't leave it! This is . . . Do you have any idea what it was like to get these people to come to the table?

ISAAC
(overlapping)

This is a negotiation! You don't know the first thing about it!

MARTIN

This is not a negotiation!

LOUIS
(exploding, to Martin)

Take it! We take it! Tell them yes!
(to Isaac)

I'm not schlepping one more fucking block with you! Are you fucking nuts?

Isaac looks at Louis—a man betrayed.

INT. ISAAC'S HOUSE. LIVING ROOM. NIGHT.

ANGLE ON ISAAC *walking into the room. He's wearing a pair of red-striped flannel pajamas, and is carrying the publisher's guide.*

> MARTIN
> *(to himself)*

I paid this.

> ISAAC
> *(perplexed)*

Martin, this Iophon Press. It's not in the publisher's guide. It's nowhere. It's not even in the phone book.

ANGLE ON MARTIN *at the desk paying bills. Worn down, exasperated. Closes his eyes.*

> MARTIN

It's new. I told you.

> ISAAC

Well then, I should maybe sit down with them and find out if they know what they're up to.

> MARTIN

You're not going to sit down with anyone, Dad.

INT. ISAAC'S HOUSE. LIVING ROOM. NIGHT.(CONTINUED).

ANGLE ON MARTIN

MARTIN

I've found these people and you're not going to blow it.

The tea kettle WHISTLES.

MARTIN

Could you get the tea?

Isaac looks down at Martin.

ISAAC

You're taking charge?

MARTIN

I'm taking charge.

Martin stares at Isaac.

ISAAC
(to self as he walks toward kettle)
Well, if you would have shown such interest six years ago, you
wouldn't have to pick up the pieces right now.

INT. ISAAC'S HOUSE. MARTIN'S ROOM. NIGHT.

*Moonlight filters in through the window. Martin is asleep on top of the
bed. The door opens offscreen, and a crack of light from the hall moves
across Martin.*

*ANGLE ON ISAAC entering in his pajamas. Martin stirs without waking.
Isaac wraps his feet with the blanket. Martin's handkerchief is lying on the
ground.*

He exits, closing the door behind him. HOLD on Martin sleeping.

INT. MARTIN'S ROOM. MORNING.

Martin asleep. Offscreen the sound of garbage trucks on the street, traffic, etc. Light pouring in. From the living room, a recording of Tristan and Isolde *is blasting to a conclusion.*

ANGLE ON ISAAC bursting into the room, in his pajamas. He is holding an old photograph.

> ISAAC
> *(bewildered)*
> I don't understand this, Martin, what the hell is going on? Who is this? Who the hell is that in there?

He holds the picture up to Martin, who is startled awake.

> MARTIN
> What?

> ISAAC
> Who the hell is that in there? There's no name on the back! I don't know who it is!

He thrusts the picture in front of Martin, who blinks at it, and looks at Isaac.

> MARTIN
> It's Herman.

> ISAAC
> It's what?

MARTIN

It's Uncle Herman.

ISAAC

(looks at the picture, terrified)

What?

MARTIN

It's your cousin Herman. You came over with him.

Isaac nods and wanders out of the room. Martin looks around, fully awake by now, and gets out of bed.

ISAAC

(exiting)

My cousin Herman . . .

MARTIN

Jesus. What time is it? I can't be late again.

He darts around the room, gathering his clothes.

INT. ISAAC'S HOUSE. LIVING ROOM. MORNING.

ANGLE ON MARTIN at the front door—about to leave. He stops.

INT. LIVING ROOM. MORNING

ANGLE ON Isaac over at a table filled with framed photographs.

CLOSE UP ON PHOTOGRAPH of a group family portrait from the late forties.

ANGLE ON ISAAC peering down from over the frame. A look of incomprehension across his face. Martin in the background opening the door, rushing out, not paying any attention to Isaac.

ISAAC IN LONG SHOT: He puts the photograph down on the mantelpiece and picks up another one, and stares at it. Silence. After a beat, Martin reappears in the frame.

MARTIN

Dad. You need to see a doctor. That was an episode. You just had an episode.

ANGLE ON ISAAC

ISAAC

Come here. Come, come, come. Come here.

He points to a picture from the fifties.

ISAAC

So tell me something. Who is that? That is Norman Nathanson.

He goes on pointing to other people in other pictures on the mantelpiece, in rapid succession.

ISAAC

And this one is Alex, and Sylvia, and Jonah Berger and Jonah's stupid kurveh mother with a Ph.D. in pedantry, and here, that's Clayton Broomer the prick from the *New Yorker*, and this one, oh look who's there, Abrahamson, the lawyer so tell me you think I need a doctor now? And who is this? This is Alvin Green, the lousy columnist from Baltimore. So go back to your flower arranging and be a good boy.

Martin has already turned around and is headed down the stairs. Isaac goes back to the pictures.

> ### ISAAC
> I know all you people.

He picks up one of the photos, stares at it, and sits down.

INT. DINING ROOM. DAY.

Morning light streams in. Isaac is in pajamas. Isaac carrying a tray with dry toast and tea to the table.

ANGLE ON MARTIN escorting a middle-aged Latino woman, ESME, in to meet Isaac. She has a dour look about her.

> ### MARTIN
> Dad. This is Esme. Esme, Isaac Geldhardt.

> ### ESME
> Good morning. Good morning.

Isaac just nods. Martin leads Esme into the kitchen, talking as he crosses with her.

> ### MARTIN
> (offscreen)
> Okay. This is most important.
> *(walking; to Esme)*
> He takes one-half of one of these in the morning— one-half
> and we need to keep count, because sometimes he forgets.

IN THE KITCHEN: Martin is showing Esme prescription pill bottles.

ISAAC

(listening; coming into kitchen)

Excuse me, she doesn't need to know this. Why are you telling her all this? I thought she was just here to clean . . . ?

MARTIN

Well, since she's going to be here anyway . . .

ISAAC

(turns to Esme, smiles, gracious)

My son misrepresents my needs.

ANGLE ON ISAAC, RETURNING TO DINING ROOM: *Opening the pill bottle, he takes one pill.*

ISAAC

There are some very nice sponges under that sink.

MARTIN

(crossing dining room with Esme)

Let me show you where to put your coat.

ISAAC

Oh, by the way, you like some brisket? There's brisket for lunch. You want some?

ESME

Uh-huh.

He opens the second bottle, takes out a pill, and with his knife attempts to cut it in half, but just crumples it into powder instead, and brushes the mess onto the floor. Isaac tosses the open bottle and its contents out the open window, and goes back to his tea and toast.

INT. ISAAC'S APARTMENT. LIVING ROOM/UPPER HALLWAY.
NIGHT.

Isaac dances alone in the living room, watched by Martin on the stairwell.

INT. ISAAC'S APARTMENT. LIVING ROOM. DAY.

ESME is vacuuming in the living room while Isaac sits by the window, in the wing-backed chair. Isaac looks in the direction of an empty chair.

ANGLE ON the crates of books that are now gone. We hear the sound of Isaac's voice over the vacuum cleaner, and as we move in, his voice becomes more audible, and he seems to be addressing an imaginary person. As his monologue progresses, the camera pans around and we see from Isaac's POV, in what had been the empty chair, a striking-looking European woman in her forties, RENA KREEGER GELDHART, in whom one sees Sarah and Aaron.

ISAAC

So, anyway, do you want to know who I saw today? That guy, you know the doctor, the one that you didn't want to go to because you had to have a lady touch you in these places, what was his name again, no, no, not him . . . the *father*, yes the one who told me that I had to stop smoking because I would be dead in five years, well you want to know what he looks like today? He looks like *he* died five years ago, yes, he's got . . . he's white . . . he's all white—he's ashen with a liver spot and he was walking with this woman, this succubus on his arm, no, this is not the same one, this is another, well, maybe it's not another one, maybe it's the same one but with new orange hair sticking out of a bag for a hat . . . like a pastry bag . . . you know? You would have known how to handle this situation. But me, I just stood there and I said, "Aha, so it's you."

We realize that the vacuuming has stopped.

ANGLE ON THE CLEANING LADY standing over Isaac, looking down at him.

> CLEANING LADY
>
> You said something?

> ISAAC
> *(dismissing her)*
> Well, it's very clean here, so just go downstairs please.

She looks at him for a beat.

INT. CHARTWELL BOOKSTORE. MADISON AVE. DAY.

Christmas time. Decorations abound. Customers in shop wear heavy coats and hats.

ANGLE ON YOUNG BOOK CLERK

Isaac peering down at the new book table. He does a thorough scan, clearly looking for a particular title.

> ISAAC
> *(to himself, shaking his head)*
> Where the hell could it be . . . This is crazy, this is absolutely crazy.

YOUNG BOOK CLERK
(approaching helpfully)
Can I help you, Mr. Geldhart?

ISAAC
Yes, yes. My book, the Foukold.

He holds out his hands in a "where is it" gesture?

CLERK
The Fuckold?

ISAAC
No. Louis Foukold. *The Science of Genocide.*

CLERK
Let's take a look.

He goes to the computer, followed by Isaac.

CLERK
(confused)
Foukold is F-U-C-K-O . . .

As the clerk punches in various letters, tries various things, not coming up with anything.

ISAAC
(annoyed; looking around at the tables)
F-O-U-K-O-L-D, Foukold . . . Tell me something, are you still
in the business of selling books or what?

He wanders back to the shelves.

ISAAC

Maybe you keep the more . . . expensive books in a special . . .
place or the—

*Isaac goes behind the counter, looking at the expensive books on the shelf.
He is utterly baffled.*

CLERK

I'm sorry Mr. Geldhardt, I'm just not coming up with anything.
Are you sure of the title?

*ANGLE ON ISAAC thumbing through a William Wegman book, shaking
his head.*

ISAAC
(mumbling)

Look at this, he's always putting clothes on that poor dog, he
says he loves her but she looks very unhappy to me . . .

CLERK
(still at computer)

There is a lot of genocide, but no science of.

Isaac looks up from the Wegman.

ISAAC

What?

He sees a pile of Tiepolo books, and gasps in pleasure.

ISAAC
(picks one up, whispers)

I had this one but I lost it!

He pages through it lovingly, the Foukold completely forgotten.

103

CLERK

Are you sure it's in release yet?

ISAAC

(starting out the door, holds up the Tiepolo)
Please, put this on my account.

He wanders out of the store, shaking his head in wonderment at the Tiepolo book, and walks away. The clerk looks on.

CLERK

Mr. Geldhardt?

INT. TAILORS. FITTING ROOM. DAY.

Through the window, we see a rainy, wintery day. Isaac is standing on a
tailor's box, being fitted for a chalk stripe suit by a dapper tailor. He is
still examining the Tiepolo book as the tailor fits his cuff. There are pins
and darts in the back—the suit is barely constructed.

ISAAC

Oh yes, this is magnificent. Look at this, the exuberance. Triumphant.

TAILOR

Is this short enough Mr. Geldhart?

ISAAC

Look at this. Look at that.
I mean, you don't see it like this, of course, in Venice.
You see it like this,

Isaac holds the book way up over his head.

ISAAC

It's on the ceiling, and you walk in and you see this exquisite
fresco—

TAILOR

Mr. Geldhart, may I hold that for you for just a second until
we finish?

ISAAC

Oh, sure.

*He hands Dennis the book, which the tailor places on the floor next to
him.*

TAILOR

Now, is this short enough Mr. Geldhardt?

*ANGLE ON ANOTHER CUSTOMER exiting a dressing room, Isaac
sees his reflection in the three-quarters mirror.*

ISAAC
(pointing at the man)
Oh my God. That's it! That's it. You remember, the ones I was
talking about! He's got them, exactly the ones.

Isaac steps down off the box, over Dennis.

*ISAAC'S POV: The customer exiting the tailor shop and opening an um-
brella.*

*ANGLE ON ISAAC following the other customer out onto the street,
leaving Dennis the tailor simply kneeling on the floor, beside the Tiepolo
book.*

EXT. ART'S CLUB RESTAURANT. DAY.

ANGLE ON CUSTOMER *entering.*

INT. ART'S CLUB RESTAURANT. DAY.

The customer is seated at a table. Isaac enters the restaurant behind him, relieved to have finally caught up.

ANGLE ON ISAAC *sitting opposite the customer in his incomplete suit— chalk marks, pins—people take notice.*

ANGLE ON *the startled-looking customer. The* CUSTOMER *ignores Isaac, that being the usual best course of action in these cases. The customer tries to read the menu.*

INT. ART'S CLUB RESTAURANT. DAY.

ANGLE ON TABLE: *Isaac leans in to speak to the man.*

> ISAAC
>
> Excuse me, but I had to run after you looking like this because you are wearing the most magnificent pair of shoes. Do you know how long I have been looking for those shoes? I mean it's one piece of leather, right? Just one piece . . .

The customer looks to the maitre d', who is standing helplessly beside Isaac.

> MAITRE D'
>
> Is there something I can help you with, Sir?

ISAAC

You see, the first time I saw that shoe was at the Sacher Hotel in the lobby, I mean I didn't want to go there, but my wife— I want to buy his shoes.

Isaac looks at the hapless customer.

ISAAC

I'm not daring to hope that we are the same size.

He looks under the table.

ISAAC
(looking at the feet)
No, you look like a wide, actually I could have them copied . . .

The maitre d' has summoned help from the waitstaff.

In the background, a waitress is at the bar, on the phone, obviously calling the police.

MAITRE D'

Sir. Please. If I may ask you to leave this gentleman.

ISAAC
(ignores this)
What I suggest is for the deal that after lunch . . .

MAITRE D'

Sir. You really are going to have to leave now or I'll have to call the police.

ISAAC

. . . what I suggest is after lunch that we go to Bergdorf's and you can choose whatever suits your fancy and that way you won't feel . . .

MAITRE D'
(to customer)
Sir, I'm sorry, if you'll just follow me, I'll show you the—

The customer rises, nodding, and Isaac rises with him, knocking over a flower arrangement. The maitre d' reaches over Isaac to right it, and Isaac pushes her away.

ISAAC
(shouting)
What are you doing? Is there something—please. Madame, this is inappropriate.

He stands over the table, glaring at the maitre d'. The restaurant is very quiet.

ISAAC
What? What?

INT. TV STUDIO. SARAH'S DRESSING ROOM. SINK. DAY

A YOUNG MAN, PETER, with the unmistakable look of an unemployed handsome actor, and Sarah in passionate embrace on the floor. Peter is very aggressive. Sarah is willing but finds the interlude awkward.

INT. TV STUDIO. SARAH'S DRESSING ROOM. DAY.

ANGLE ON EMILY THE DOG watching from her doggy bed.

INT. TV STUDIO. SARAH'S DRESSING ROOM. DAY.

> SARAH
>
> Ouch. Ouch. You're on my pigtail . . . ouch. Peter, I just did this stupid makeup . . .

Peter keeps kissing her, very passionately.

> SARAH
>
> Honestly, I can't, Peter, honestly . . . ouch!

> PETER
> *(backing away)*
>
> Why are you so uptight?

> SARAH
>
> Why are you always trying to screw me on the floor? These are working hours, I am working here. There are teamsters out there teaming around us, you're just . . .

> PETER
>
> I'm what? Immature? I'm not some fifty-something art fag?

> SARAH
> *(laughing)*
>
> Oh, yeah. There we go.

> PETER
>
> I don't have great funny stories where I tilt my head and tell people what's what . . .

INT. TV STUDIO. SARAH'S DRESSING ROOM. DAY.

SARAH

What? Peter. You think that I'm still kissing with Max? Is that it? Because come on please, get off it.

PETER

I ask you to softball in the park, to league, and it's like I asked you to some toxic dump.

The following goes on under Peter.

SARAH

I know, I know. Peter, sweetie, listen this dog is going to take a shit right here in this room and I have a shot to do. I have to go sing a song about trichinosis. So . . .
                    (beat, pleading)

PETER

I'm not your boy. I'm not your dog boy.

SARAH

                    (incredulous; sort of amused)
My *dog* boy?

There is a KNOCK on the dressing room door. Max enters.

MAX

Your father's been arrested.
                    (he points out)
Aaron's on the phone.

INT. TV STUDIO. DAY.

ANGLE ON SARAH *running out of the dressing room, toward the floor manager's phone.*

MAX

You have two more shots. You're not leaving now. Tell him you're not leaving now.

INT. POLICE STATION. DAY. LATE AFTERNOON. HEAVY RAIN

Isaac descends the police station steps, followed by Sarah and Aaron.

SARAH

Dad, talk to me.

ISAAC

Send me a bill for the bail, I don't have my checks.

SARAH

Dad, stop! What happened.

Aaron nods. Sarah watches.

ISAAC

I'll get a taxi. That's all. I'm fine. Thank you.

Aaron nods. He can't really look at Isaac.

SARAH
(still under the awning)
You think what you do has no effect on us?

Isaac runs out of the station into the rain.

AARON

Let him go, Sarah.

Isaac reenters the station and comes up to Aaron.

ISAAC

What did you do with my books?

Aaron stares at Isaac.

ISAAC

You thought you'd get away with it, huh?

Aaron, surprised, says nothing.

ISAAC

You're getting sentimental, Aaron. Not good for business.

AARON

No. Not at all.

Isaac looks at Aaron for a moment, nods, and suddenly lunges at Aaron, pushing him onto the floor and out the police station.

ISAAC
(screaming)

You shit-ass!

Sarah runs out, trying to pull Isaac off Aaron and trying to keep Aaron from hitting his father.

ANGLE ON AARON AND ISAAC *struggling.*

SARAH
(going to Isaac to help)
Stop it. Daddy. Aaron. Stop it . . . Stop.
(to police)
Do something, please!

Two policemen come and separate them. Isaac starts to walk away.

ISAAC
Leave me alone.

AARON
(calling after Isaac, who stops)
You deserve everything that's happening to you, Isaac.

Isaac continues to walk away.

INT. ISAAC'S APARTMENT. SPRING DAY.

Angle on Isaac sitting in the chair by the window.

ANGLE ON MARTIN coming out of the kitchen. He is extremely anxious and seems overwhelmed. He has on a jacket. He does not look at all well. Very pale, clammy.

MARTIN
Come on, Isaac. Put on your tie, she's going to be here any minute.

ISAAC
Maybe she won't come. I'm telling you, Martin, you can't run a place this big with only a woman who comes in once a week from Belize . . .

MARTIN

Dad . . .

ISAAC

The dust in this place . . . it's like a nuclear winter in here . . .
You have to take three showers a day.

MARTIN

(exhausted)

It's the social worker. That's today.

ISAAC

Please, do you think I'm an idiot? Today's the maid. Thursday's
the Sotheby lady.

MARTIN

It's the psychiatric social worker. That's today. You agreed to
this.

ISAAC

Do I look to you like a man who doesn't have a calendar?
Thursday is the social worker. Today is Tuesday. The cleaning.
Please!

MARTIN

Today, actually, is in point of fact, Thursday.

There is a silence.

ISAAC

Without Miss Barzakian how'm I supposed to know my appointments? It was idiotic to have consented to this in the first
place.

MARTIN

It would help if you knew what days of the week it was.

ISAAC

What for? Just a slab of days. Tell me something, Martin, what do you do? You go back to Aaron? With reports?

MARTIN
(suddenly suspicious)
What did you mean the Sotheby lady . . . What were you talking about before?

ISAAC

You don't know everything about my business affairs, thank God.

MARTIN

There's nothing left to sell, Isaac. You can't be going to auction houses, talking to Sotheby's. Jesus.

ISAAC
(sly)
You really think there's nothing. Well, don't worry. There's plenty. The Sotheby people know just what I've got.

MARTIN

It's the social worker, Dad. And it wasn't my idea.

ISAAC
(scornful)
No, of course not, but if Aaron says that I'm incompetent there's got to be something to it, right?

MARTIN

Now's your chance to prove there isn't.

ISAAC

(crossing to the window)

I'd like to get the hell out of this town. A building blew up
across the park. Apparently there was a cloud of asbestos. Now
there's cancer for everyone. The whole street was a freak show.

MARTIN

Yes, I know, we've talked about this.

ISAAC

(at the window, looks out)

I always hated that park. You need a key to get in and there's
never anyone there.

MARTIN

I used to always be there. I loved that park. I still have the key.

*Martin comes over to the window, and stands beside Isaac, looking out.
Isaac looks at Martin, who is sweating, still in his jacket.*

ISAAC

Why do you dress like some sort of Paul Bunyon character. I
mean, what's with that jacket?

*There is a BUZZ. The door. Martin looks out the window at the front
door.*

MARTIN

(turns back to Isaac)

Dad, let me give you some advice. You just answer "yes" or

"no." You don't have to do the whole Isaac Geldhart show. It's not required. These people, they don't let you off on charm. They don't even get it—

ISAAC

I get it. Quit your carping! Standing here giving me instructions like I was in your photosynthesis class or something.

Martin runs down the stairs and opens the door.

INT. ISAAC'S HOUSE. HALL/STAIRWAY. DAY.

ANGLE ON MARTIN standing in doorway, opening door on a woman in her forties, MARTHA HACKETT.

MARTHA

Hi, I'm Martha Hackett.

MARTIN

Listen, I know you came all the way here, but I don't think this is the greatest time.

MARTHA

Well, the department is swamped. To get one of these appointments, and to get someone to come to the house, it's very difficult. Why drag it on?

INT. ISAAC'S HOUSE. LIVING ROOM. DAY.

MARTHA HACKETT'S POV: Isaac sits at his desk pretending to read.

MARTIN

Dad.

Isaac turns, gets up, very courtly, and comes to the threshold of the living room.

ISAAC

Isaac Geldhart.

He holds out his hand. Martha steps forward.

MARTHA

Yes. Martha Hackett.

They shake hands.

ISAAC

Let me get the woman to bring you some coffee . . .

Isaac heads through the upper hallway toward the dining room. Martin cuts him off. Isaac remains in the upper hallway.

MARTIN
(looking at Isaac)

No, I'll do it.

Martin goes off, into the kitchen.

ISAAC
(catching the glance)

Oh of course, it's not Tuesday. It's Thursday. She has a tendency not to show. Also she ain't listed so I'm fucked.

118

INT. ISAAC'S APARTMENT. UPPER HALLWAY. DAY.

ANGLE ON MARTHA: impassive, watching Isaac.

ISAAC

Forgive me. I'm trying to be competent. That's the thing you
need to know, is it not?

MARTHA

Mr. Geldhart. Nothing is being determined here.

ISAAC

Oh, forgive me, I thought something was being determined
here.

MARTHA

No. This is a process. No one person can make a dispensation
or come to a conclusion.

ISAAC

No one person? That means there are more of you to come? A
tribunal?

MARTHA

It's not that bad.

ISAAC
(suddenly furious)
They send a woman to my house to see if I am wacko and
nothing is being determined here? The-the-the paperwork that
has come flying into this house from all the places . . .

MARTHA

Mr. Geldhart . . . you don't have to . . . worry . . .

ISAAC

I don't have to what? Why don't you just tell me exactly what
I have to do?

INT. ISAAC'S APARTMENT. UPPER HALLWAY. DAY.

ANGLE ON MARTIN *entering upper hallway. He has a tray with coffee
and cream. He is stricken.*

MARTIN

Dad! Dad!

ISAAC

Martin, do you think I would really subject myself to this pa-
tronizing . . .
                    (rushing to Martin, grabs his arm)
Look at what they brought me . . . Look what they sent me . . .

MARTHA

(to Martin)
It's okay. Why don't you just leave us for a bit.

ISAAC

Why don't you both leave me alone. Do you think anyone
wants to be seen this way? I mean it's so fucking vulgar!

MARTHA

(to Martin, who still is holding the tray, immobilized)
It's all right.

She gently takes the tray from him. His hands are shaking, as are the cups.

MARTIN
(*pointing toward dining room*)
I'll be there.

ANGLE ON MARTIN: *going into the dining room. Still listening to Isaac and Martha, in the other room. He sits on a stool.*

ISAAC
(*snorts derisively*)
You'll be there.

MARTHA
He told me you might be a little cranky.

INT. ISAAC'S HOUSE. DINING ROOM. DAY.

ANGLE ON MARTIN *sitting on stool listening.*

ISAAC
(*offscreen*)
A little *cranky?*

ISAAC
(*offscreen to Martin, yelling*)
That's your brilliant analysis of my situation here? A *little bit cranky?* Fuck you!

Martin closes his eyes. He is sweating, clearly unwell.

INT. ISAAC'S HOUSE. UPPER HALLWAY. DAY.

Martha holding up a placating hand to Isaac, who is glowering.

MARTHA

Mr. Geldhart . . . he didn't mean . . . to be insulting.

ISAAC

So. Tell me then, how are things at Sotheby's?

MARTHA

Sotheby's?

ANGLE ON ISAAC IN LIVING ROOM opening the portfolio in which he keeps his collection of illustrated letters.

ISAAC

Come on, I know you have other places to go, and we're both
busy people, and you have other treasures to plunder.

MARTHA

I'm not from Sotheby's, I'm from Social Services.

ANGLE ON ISAAC looking up from his letter portfolio at her. He takes this in, and nods.

MARTHA

Please, Mr. Geldhart, understand, your son Aaron and your
daughter Sarah have suggested that competency hearings be in-
itiated because you have demonstrated a credible inability to
manage your own affairs.

ISAAC

Did the woman give you coffee?

MARTHA

All I have to do is ask you a few questions.

ISAAC

Okay. Shoot.

MARTHA

What city, state, and country are we living in?

ISAAC

Are you kidding me?

MARTHA

It's a perfectly reasonable question.

ISAAC

Next.

MARTHA

(looks over her list of questions—none are any better—goes to her notes)
Do you know . . . ? Your medication is . . . ?

ISAAC

I stopped taking it, I couldn't read. That, I could not accept.
(suddenly bright)
Enough of this, right? Now let me show you the collection.
Mind you, it's understood from the get-go, you take the entire
collection.

Isaac is opening up the portfolios.

ISAAC

I can't bear to think of this being divvied up, split up, all over
town.

MARTHA

I am not from an auction house.

ISAAC

I have a letter from Hitler. Adolph Hitler.

(beat)

It's a postcard actually. He painted this. A little watercolor of a burnt-out church.

ANGLE ON ISAAC showing Martha the Hitler postcard.

ISAAC

There was a Jewish shop owner in the town who thought that young Adolf had talent. So he gave him his materials for free.

Isaac stares at the postcard.

ISAAC

What do you think? There is something here, is there not?

MARTHA

Do you really think I'm from an auction house?

ISAAC

(exploding)

I know exactly where you're from and what you're trying to do to me, you fucking cunt! You know the time. You know what time it is! You know all the times! All you fucking people know exactly what to do to me!

INT. ISAAC'S HOUSE. DINING ROOM. DAY.

Martin has rolled up his sleeve, and is examining a bruise on his forearm, sniffling a little. He realizes his nose is bleeding. His face is glistening with sweat. Woozy.

> MARTIN
> *(weakly)*

Dad, Dad.

> ISAAC

Get out of my house! Both of you!

Martin walks unsteadily toward the living room, then crumples in a heap on the floor, right in front of Isaac, at his feet.

INT. NEW YORK HOSPITAL. WAITING ROOM. DAY.

A waiting area off intensive care. Aaron and Sarah sit beside Dr. BART KRAMER, who is exhausted, his head in his hands. Sarah is quietly crying. Aaron speaks over her, to Kramer. Isaac sits off to one side, by himself.

> AARON

How could it have gotten to this point? I mean . . . without somebody catching it. Doctor, I'm not blaming you . . . you've always been great . . . but didn't you . . . call him or something? To check up on him?

> KRAMER

Actually, the patient does the calling if they notice any trouble.

> AARON

What about follow-ups? You don't do follow-ups?

> SARAH

Aaron—

> KRAMER

As far as I know, your brother had been terribly careful with himself.

AARON

So how could this have happened? Why wouldn't he call?

KRAMER

I gotta tell you: I don't think he wanted to.

AARON

What does that mean?

SARAH

(*very emotional*)

For God's sake, Aaron. He didn't want to.

ANGLE ON ISAAC *getting up and walking away unnoticed by the others.*

INT. NEW YORK HOSPITAL. HALLWAY. DAY.

He wanders down the hall, peering into rooms.

ISAAC'S POV: *Martin in a bed, unconscious, hooked up to IVs, and monitors in the near dark.*

INT. NEW YORK HOSPITAL. HOSPITAL ROOM. NIGHT.

ANGLE ON ISAAC *watching Martin for a moment. Isaac looks at the monitors, as though trying to comprehend them. He stands beside the bed, and fixes the blanket around Martin's feet. Stands there.*

ANGLE ON DR. KRAMER *standing in the doorway, looking at Isaac, who has his hands on the blanket, stroking Martin's feet. Isaac is looking up at the monitors.*

> KRAMER

Isaac. You can't be back here.

> ISAAC
> *(indicates monitors)*

Which one is the special one? The most important one to watch?

> KRAMER

They're all important.

> ISAAC

He didn't have these last time, he was with the awful orange flowers and the cars on the wall. What kind of people make vinyl wallpaper?

> KRAMER

We really can't stay here, Isaac.

> ISAAC
> *(looks at Martin)*

But he's big now. He's in charge now.

Isaac starts to walk away from Martin, looks back at him, and Dr. Kramer leads him out.

HOLD on Dr. Kramer leading Isaac down the hall of the hospital.

EXT. CEMETERY. DAY.

LONGSHOT: Isaac, Aaron, Sarah, Miss Barzakian, Louis, Val, Bernard, Martin's group of students, and a Rabbi all standing around a freshly dug grave. Isaac has the shovel in his hand. *IN LONG-SHOT, we see it passed from person to person, each one shovels a clump of dirt onto the coffin. Each time there is a resounding thump, which grows duller, as more dirt is piled on.*

INT. ISAAC'S HOUSE. DAY.

A little gathering of mourners in the living room, including those at the burial and the rabbi. Louis sits with Miss Barzakian. Isaac stands at the window, looking out.

ANGLE ON ISAAC now sitting in the chair by the window. On his lap is the portfolio of illustrated letters. He is looking down at them in the sunlight. He pulls out the Hitler postcard.

INT. ISAAC'S HOUSE. DINING ROOM. DAY.

ANGLE ON SARAH in dining room, sitting with Peter, her boyfriend, who is holding her hand. They sit silently at the dining room table.

> SARAH
> *(looks at Peter)*
Is this awful for you?

Sarah looks at Peter and smiles. What she sees is a kind and genuine man.

> PETER
> *(looking at Isaac by the window)*
Sarah. You're really going to have to talk to him. I know it's none of my business. But nobody's talked to him.

CUT TO AARON talking with other guests.

INT. ISAAC'S HOUSE. LIVING ROOM. DAY.

ANGLE ON ISAAC *rising and starting out of the living room. Miss Barzakian stands in his path. He looks through her, and moves on.*

INT. ISAAC'S HOUSE. HALLWAY. DAY.

ANGLE ON ISAAC *going down the stairs into Martin's room. THE CAMERA follows him.*

INT. ISAAC'S HOUSE. MARTIN'S ROOM. DAY.

Isaac sits on the bed. He looks at the folded blanket. He lights a candle on the windowsill, then takes the Hitler postcard from his jacket pocket and sets it on fire.

ANGLE ON ISAAC *burning the postcard, his face illuminated by the flame. He places the postcard in the candle dish where it burns to a smoking ember.*

ANGLE ON SARAH AND AARON *in the doorway, watching Isaac.*

> AARON
>
> Dad, what's that? What are you doing?

> ISAAC
>
> Nothing.

He looks at them for a moment.

> SARAH
>
> Are you all right?

ISAAC

Would you like to go for a walk in the park?

SARAH

Now?

AARON

Dad. We have guests.

ISAAC

Come on. They're doing okay. Louis is keeping them enter-
tained.
(beat)
Come on.

ANGLE ON ISAAC *going to the bureau, to a little saucer with keys in it.*
Isaac scoops up all the keys. Aaron and Sarah follow him out the front
door.

EXT. ISAAC'S HOUSE/GRAMERCY PARK. DAY.

Isaac walking with the kids, searching through his handful of keys. Aaron
and Sarah catch up to him.

ISAAC

I don't know exactly which key it is.

AARON

(*peering over Isaac's shoulder, points.*)
I think it's this one.

They're at the park gate.

EXT. GRAMERCY PARK. DAY.

Isaac, Sarah, and Aaron stand at the gate. He tries the key. It works. He opens the door and they enter the empty park.

ANGLE ON ISAAC AND AARON AND SARAH entering Gramercy Park. Sarah reaches behind them to close the gate.

> ISAAC
>
> No. Leave it open. Someone fun might drop by.

Isaac looks around the park.

> ISAAC
>
> Aaron. You punched a little boy over by that fountain. I was so surprised. I had a little warrior boy. And you. I came here and sat on that bench when you got laid in our apartment for the first time. I just sat here. On this bench. I thought that I would quite literally die. *(beat)*

They sit down on a bench, facing the apartment.

> ISAAC
>
> But this was Martin's park. I used to watch him from the window until it got dark. *(beat)* Then I'd have to come down and find him.

Hold on Isaac, Sarah, and Aaron in the park, in the gathering dusk.

EXT. GRAMERCY PARK. DUSK.

ANGLE ON PETER entering through the gate of the park. Sarah rises to greet him. Then Louis and Miss Barzakian enter the park with Val as we continue to PULL BACK to the apartment window and into the apartment.

EXT. GRAMERCY PARK. DUSK.

LONGSHOT CONTINUING; PULLING BACK POV: *From the apartment, a gathering of people surround Isaac, Aaron, and Sarah in the gathering dusk.*

SLOW FADE TO BLACK
THE END

CAST AND CREDIT LIST

Miramax Films
Presents
A Film by Daniel Sullivan

Tony Goldwyn

Timothy Hutton

Sarah Jessica Parker

Ron Rifkin

THE SUBSTANCE OF FIRE

Gil Bellows

Elizabeth Franz

Ronny Graham

Debra Monk

Roger Rees

and Eric Bogosian

Casting by
Meg Simon, CSA

Costume Designer
Jess Goldstein

Music by
Joseph Vitarelli

Editor
Pamela Martin

Production Designer
John Lee Beatty

Director of Photography
Robert Yeoman

Co-Producer
Lemore Syvan

Produced by
Jon Robin Baitz
Randy Finch
Ron Kastner

Screenplay by
Jon Robin Baitz

Based upon his play

Directed by
Daniel Sullivan

CAST
(In Order of Appearance)

Young Isaac Geldhart	Benjamin Ungar
Isaac Geldhart	Ron Rifkin
Old Printer	Tom McDermott
Otto the Printer	George Morfogen
Cora Cahn	Lee Grant
Aaron Geldhart	Tony Goldwyn
Mr. Otani Junior	Andrew Pang
Mr. Otani Senior	Edmund Ikeda
Miss Barzakian	Elizabeth Franz
Val Chenard	Gil Bellows
Gene Byck	Eric Bogosian
Louis Foukold	Ronny Graham
Martin Geldhart	Timothy Hutton
Stewart	John Sullivan
Rachel	Sophia Salguero
Sarah Geldhart	Sarah Jessica Parker
Peter	Jon Patrick Walker
Max	Roger Rees

Nurse	Viola Davis
Dr. Bernard Kramer	David S. Howard
Young Martin	Gregory Burke
Mr. Musselblatt	Adolph Green
Mr. Cox	William Cain
New Receptionist	Alec Mapa
Miquel	Edgar Martinez
Book Binder	John Christopher Jones
Mr. McCormack Senior	Dick Latessa
Mr. McCormack Junior	Patrick Page
Rizzoli Book Buyer	Kate Forbes
Esme	Gloria Irizarry
Rena Geldhart	Barbara Eda-Young
Young Book Clerk	Matt McGrath
Dennis the Tailor	Jose Ramon Rosario
Customer with Shoes	William Meisle
Maitre D'	Gina Torres
Martha Hackett	Debra Monk
Rabbi	Rabbi Marc Schneier
Line Producer	Lemore Syvan
Production Manager	A. John Rath
First Assistant Director	Jeff Lazar
Second Assistant Director	John M. Tyson
Production Sound Mixer	Pawel Wdowczak
Boom Operator	Laurel Ann Bridges
Script Supervisor	Christine Gee
First Assistant Camera	Storn "Norp" Peterson
Second Assistant Camera	Bart A. Blaise
Camera PA	Matthew Flannery
Still Photographer	Bill Foley
Gaffer	Toshiaki Ozawa
Best Boy Electric	Antonio M. Rossi
Electrics	Kate M. Phelan
	John C. Tanzer
Key Rigging Gaffer	John Billeci

Key Grip	Daniel Beaman
Best Boy Grips	Jonathan Kovel
	Sean M. Donovan
Grips	James J. Ferris
	Andrew Montlack
	Joe Baccari
	Patrick Donovan
Key Rigging Grip	Joe Foley
Supervising Sound Editor	Steve Hamilton
Re-Recording Mixer	Reilly Steele
Sound Editors	Mary Ellen Porto
	Juan Carlos Martinez
ADR Editor	Steve Silkensen
Foley Editor	Andrew Kris
Foley Artist	Linda Russo
Audio Post Coordinator	Jeanette King
Assistant Editor	Simon Allen
Apprentice Editors	May Kuckro
	Jake A. Mosler
Assistant Sound Editor	Joe Cimino
Score Produced by	Joseph Vitarelli
Orchestrations	Jorge Del Barrio
Music Recording	Daniel Wallin
	Nicholas Viterelli
Music Preparation	Ken Gruberman
Music Editors	Allan K. Rosen
	David Carbonara
Music Contractor	Bill Hughes
Music Production Coordinator	Paula Hoppe
Set Decorator	Shelley Barclay
Art Director	Mark Ricker
Graphic Designer	Mary Ellen Carroll
Art Department Coordinator	Alex Westerman
Leadman	Jeremiah Small
Construction Coordinator	James Chinlund
Scenic Charge	Constance L. Schlier

Scenic Artist	Shana M. Burns
Prop Masters	Ben Barraud
	Stuart Montgomery
Additional Props	Caitlin A. Hahn
	Jeremy E. Buhler
Wardrobe Supervisor	Terri Purcell
Assistant Costume Designer	Katherine B. Roth
Wardrobe Assistant	Michael Zecker
Key Make-Up and Hair	Todd Thomas
	Tracy Warbin
Additional Make-Up & Hair	Katherine E. Morgan
Locations Manager	David Martin
Asst. Locations Manager	Carey De Palma
Unit Manager	Michael Johnson
Locations Scout	Maria Essen
Production Coordinator	Melissa M. Marr
Asst. Production Coordinator	Juliet D'Annibale
Production Accountant	Pam Cheney
Asst. Production Accountant	Michael Rath
Add'l. 1st Asst. Director	Julian Petrillo
2nd 2nd Asst. Director	Linda Krantz
Assistant to Director	Christina Rosati
Assistants to Producers	Matthew Elefant
	Howie Statland
Legal Services	Jay S. Harris, Esq.
	Hall Dickler Kent
	Friedman & Wood LLP.
Medical Consultant	Bernard Kruger, MD.
Casting Associate	Stephanie Corsalini
Extras Casting	Amerifilm Casting, Inc.
	Meredith Jacobson Marciano
Dialect Coach	Deborah Hecht

Key Set PA	Jennifer Truelove
Set PA's	Deanna Leslie
	Will McCormack
	Mary Jackson
	Jonathan Goldstein
	Jody Hessel
	Scott Doorley
	Alex Raban
	Aiko Fuji
Stand-Ins	Phillip Hinch
	Adrienne Alitowski
	Raven Little
	Stephanie F. Michels
Steadicam Operator	Jacques Jouffret
Asst. Steadicam Operator	Luke Eder
Animals	Susan Jaffe of Dawn Animal Agency
Special Effects	Drew Jiritano
Special Effects Assistant	John Stifanich
Pyrotechnician	Wyatt Baker
Stuntmen	Douglas C. Crosby
	Blaise Corrigan
Art Department PA's	Stephanie Ferrante
	Vaughn Washington
	Beth Skoglund
	Rene Asenault
	Denise Grillo
Props PA's	Che Chisholm
	Ron Digman
	Ficre Ghebreyesus
Make-Up PA's	Maria O'Reilly
	Martin Jouffre
Wardrobe PA	Jennifer Sultan
Locations PA's	Stuart Acher
	Sujit Chawla
	Matt Whitcher

PA's	Jennifer Euston
	Deborah Friedman
	Nicole Gratson
	Jeremy Kraus
	Brian Macdonald
	Jason Savader
	Rhadi Taylor
	Steven Santos
Transportation Captain	William K. Gaskins
Drivers	Daniel W. Palmer
	Charles Hoffmann
	John Buckman
Parking PA's	Courtney Anderson
	Martin Henessee
	Reggie Henry
Caterers	Fresh Dish Catering

"SPECIAL FRIEND"
Music by Rick Baitz
Lyrics by Daniel Sullivan
Performed by Sarah Jessica Parker and Rick Baitz
Published by Rick Baitz and
One Hundred and Tenth Street Music (BMI)
© 1995

"LE PETIT POULET"
Written by Sinéad O'Connor and John Reynolds
Performed by Sinéad O'Connor
Produced by John Reynolds and Sinéad O'Connor
Courtesy of EMI Records
© 1995

"IF YOU WANNA KNOW HOW, CALL THE COW"
Music by Rick Baitz
Lyrics by Daniel Sullivan, Jon Robin Baitz, Rick Baitz
Performed by Sarah Jessica Parker
Published by Rick Baitz and
One Hundred and Tenth Street Music (BMI)
© 1995

SPECIAL THANKS

Arnold Rifkin, Jeff Robin, Cassian Elwes, Johnnie Planco,
Jonathan Olson, George Lane and The William Morris Agency

Harvey Weinstein, Tony Safford, David Steinberg and Miramax Films

Andre Bishop, Bernard Gersten and Lincoln Center Theatre
The Manhattan Theatre Club, Playwrights Horizons
Naked Angels Theatre Company

Tom McCormack & St. Martin's Press

Kevin Marks, Paul L. Newman, J. Michael Stremel, Sheila Mandel
Isaac Mizrahi, Marc Jacobs, Cynthia Rowley, Odd's Costume Rental
Kurt & Western Costumes

Rizzoli Books, Chartwell Booksellers, Peter Kruty Editions
City College of New York, The National Arts Club,
The Residents of Gramercy Park
New York Downtown Hospital, Vassar College, Keppler Entertainment
Premier Entertainment Services, UPP Entertainment Marketing
Dave Brown Entertainment, More Merchandising International
Doubletree Guest Suites, Harry N. Abrams, Inc.
Book Essentials Promotions, Inc., Conde Nast Publications, Inc.
The Parker Pen Company, Nat Sherman International
Benner Medical Props & Kathy Cossu, Rubbermaid, Inc.
Martex Towels, Pillowtex, Inc., Bernardaud Porcelines
Mikasa Libbey Glass, Inc., Federal Express, The Perrier Group of America
Yoo-hoo Chocolate Beverage Corp., Wild Turkey Bourbon
Glenmorangie Single Highland Malt Scotch Whiskey
Thirteen/WNET New York, Mercury Paints
Television City, Arenson Office Furnishings, Speed Graphics
Archive Photos, Mohawk Paper Mills, Inc., Alyssa DeLuccia
Jeff Kryvicky, Jesse Hollander, ABC Carpet & Home
Brooke Merrill Tinney - Dweller by the Stream Bindery, Brooklyn, NY
Lyndhurst, a property of The National Trust for Historic Preservation

Electrical and Grip Equipment	Xeno Lights, New York City
Camera Equipment	Panavision, New York
Sound Re-Recorded at	Sound One Corp., New York City
Sound Editorial Facilities	Spin Cycle Post, New York City
Music Recorded & Mixed at	Capitol Studio, Hollywood C.A.
Projectionist	Morty Kaiser
Color By	Technicolor East Coast
Technicolor Coordinator	Joe Violante
Color Timer	Mark Ginsberg
Negative Cutter	Stan and Patricia Sztaba Match/Cut Film Services
Titles and Opticals	The Effects House, Inc. John Alagna Michael Ventresco Pamela Mathis
Insurance	D.I.S.C. Insurance
Payroll Services	Entertainment Partners
Completion Bond Guarantor	Film Finances, Inc.

EDITED ON FILM

Produced on Kodak Motion Picture Film.

Filmed in Panavision	Dolby® in Selected Theatres	MPAA Motion Picture Association of America

PRINTS BY TECHNICOLOR